Predictable
Pairing

Predictable
Pairing:

The Structures of Human Atoms

by

Robert A. Ravich, M.D.
and Barbara Wyden

Peter H. Wyden/Publisher

NEW YORK

LIBRARY OF CONGRESS CATALOG CARD NUMBER: 74–15628

MANUFACTURED IN THE UNITED STATES OF AMERICA

ISBN: 0–88326–034–4

To Abe and Martha,
who gave me the gift of life,

to Ruth, who for thirty years has
been my partner in life,

to Carol and Bill, who gave so much
fullness to life,

and to Katie and Mari, who taught
me the meaning of life.

—R.A.R.

Contents

Predictable
Pairing

1

The Human Atom

What is it that goes on between two people, that emotional electricity in every pair relationship? We are all aware of it. We say, "He turns me on [or off]," "She leaves me cold," "I get bad vibrations from him," "We were attracted immediately. Sparks were flying between us." But most people consider this element something beyond their control—like the weather. They may complain about the weather, but they accept it, just as they accept the strife inherent in some pair relationships and the felicity of others.

Fifteen years ago, puzzled by the rigid yet unarticulated rules that I repeatedly observed in action between husbands and wives in crisis—even in the ultimate crisis of death—I set to work to discover what went on within the intimate relationship between a man and a woman (the nuclear pair).

I discovered a whole previously uncharted world of *predictable* interactions. I found that it is possible to *change* the vibrations within a pair (dyad) by restructuring the couple's joint behavior. Even more significant, I learned that it is possible to analyze pair* relationships very early on, even in the first week of their existence, and determine which relationships will be exciting, rewarding pairings; which will spawn extramarital sexual liaisons; which will be rather pleasant but dull; which will be sheer hell, but (unless terminated almost immediately) will seldom break up; which will inevitably end in separation or divorce; and which pairs have an excellent chance of living happily enough ever after.** I discovered that all pair relationships can be classified into eight patterns of interaction—*and that the course of pair interactions can be predicted!*

Some people are horrified at the idea of codifying interactions. They especially resist the idea that only eight categories of interaction, or couple structures, exist. They feel that there is something mechanistic and therefore threatening about this seemingly impersonal predictability.

The fact is that specific patterns of interaction are as individual as fingerprints. It is predictable that every normal baby will have ten fingers, but his fingerprints are not predictable. They are so individual that they are used

---

*In the course of my research I also discovered that my findings held true for *all* pair (one-to-one) relationships: parent and child, siblings, playmates, neighbors, teacher and student, partnerships, co-workers, employer and employee, etc.

**I say "happily enough," because I am convinced that one of the almost irresistible stresses our culture places on the institution of marriage is the expectation that this pairing should result in a "happily ever after." It won't. This is too much to expect of any relationship and too much of a burden to place on marriage. Marriage cannot and should not guarantee instant or perpetual happiness. To hope to be "happy enough" is a healthier approach.

as the ultimate means of identification. They are supremely personal. In the same way, an individual's way of interacting differs from intimate relationship to intimate relationship.

I would like to define just what I consider an intimate relationship before proceeding further. In my mind it has broader as well as narrower connotations than those that many people attach to the term.

For instance, sexuality does not necessarily connote intimacy. But the five-day-a-week, year-in, year-out interaction between Marilyn Aldrich, housewife, and Fred Harrison, mailman, who exchange "Good mornings" and comments on the weather as he delivers her letters, bills, magazines, and junk mail every morning, does constitute an intimate relationship. There is an established, ongoing interaction between Marilyn and Fred.

But, if Fred were ill one morning and a substitute mailman appeared on the doorstep, and if Marilyn Aldrich started talking to him about Fred, asking if he were seriously ill, and if she concluded by asking the substitute mailman to come in and have a cup of coffee because it was so cold, and if, after that cup of coffee and subsequent conversation, they had sexual intercourse, that would not be an intimate relationship. It would be a one-time, hit-and-run encounter. If Fred were ill for several weeks, and if the chat-coffee-intercourse sequence were repeated several times a week for those several weeks, that *would* be an intimate relationship, although quite different from the one engaged in by Fred and Marilyn.

One person can have many intimate relationships and may in each one exhibit very different aspects of his personality—indeed, so radically different that the other persons in these relationships, were they to exchange information among themselves about him, would have great difficulty in believing that they were talking about the same individual.

How a man and his first wife interact will not be the way the same man and his second wife interact, even if the marital structure falls into the same category in both cases. For there can be infinite variations within a category. And these categories and their variations can be graphically outlined with unerring accuracy—and the course of individual interactions can be forecast, just as geneticists can predict the health of a couple's offspring, with the exception that my method is more accurate than the geneticist's, because the geneticist can only cite the odds; my technique, which has become known as the Train Game, cites the facts.

My thesis about the predictability of human pairing startles most people until I show them that my findings are based on more than a decade of research involving close to one thousand couples and made possible by the development of this new diagnostic tool, the Ravich Interpersonal Game/Test—the first completely computerized method of analyzing and classifying human interaction.

I like to think of my work as a guide to closing an important gap in our knowledge of the universe. While scientists and nonscientists alike have been able to accept the fact that, like rocks, like plants, like a drop of water, the human being is a conglomeration of atoms, while they have been able to accept that unseen planets in unknown galaxies are also based on atomic structures, they have not been able to transfer this acceptance to the concept of human atoms, which follow the same logical and predictable patterns as those of the elements.

I use the term "human atom" for the nuclear pair, the couple that forms the basis of the family, indeed of civilization itself. I am convinced, on the basis of my research, that one can measure and predict the interaction within the human atom as unerringly as one can predict that two hydrogen atoms combined with one oxygen atom (H_2O) will produce a water molecule. Not only can the interaction be predicted, but the duration of that interaction—the life of the human atom—can also be predicted.

As our knowledge of analyzing and predicting pair interactions grows, I am convinced that the atomic analogies will be so striking that they will permit of no argument. In the meantime, this brief statement should suffice to explain my thesis to the lay reader. Those who are interested in further details of the human-atom concept are referred to the appendix.[1]

My concept is a return to the intuitive knowledge of Hippocrates, the great physician, who was convinced of the inevitable relationship between man and the world outside. With the growth of knowledge scientists dismissed this intuitive insight and parted ranks: the physicians looking at the human body and the physicists, like Newton and Galileo and their successors, looking at the earth and the extraterrestrial bodies. Now, science is completing the circle; we are learning that Hippocrates was right: There is a pattern and a logic to everything, including human interaction; there is order, not chaos.

One reason why the family is in such trouble today is that our knowledge of the physical world is so much more advanced than that of the intangible interactive world of pairs. We have spent vast sums of money, energy, and time investigating the physical world. We have developed ways of examining atomic structures, of actually "taking the pulse" of atomic nuclei in the cells of the human body, but until very recently no one devoted much thought, time, or energy, to say nothing of money, to the business of taking the emotional pulse of the family or of the nuclear pair who form the human atom.

The Ravich Interpersonal Game/Test has provided a concrete and significant breakthrough in our understanding of human interaction.* It involves a pair of toy electric trains, a few feet of track, a couple of switches, a barrier that can be used if desired, and a computer. To

*Lest this seem like some pleasant eccentricity or ego inflation on my part, I must point out that this diagnostic tool has been employed at the New York Hospital-Cornell Medical Center; at the Payne-Whitney Psychiatric Clinic associated with the Cornell medical complex; at McLean Hospital in Cambridge, Massachusetts; at the Gouverneur Health Services Program at Beth Israel Medical Center in New York City; at New York Medical College in New York City; at the Lutheran Medical Center in Omaha, Nebraska; at the Mental Health Clinic of Bristol Hospital in Bristol, Connecticut; at Harvard University; at Radcliffe College; at the University of Southern California; at the School of Social Welfare of the University of Wisconsin; at Loyola University in Chicago, Illinois; by the Montgomery County Retarded Children's Program in Dayton, Ohio; at Silverhill Sanatorium in New Canaan, Connecticut; and at the National Institutes of Health in Washington, D.C. The list is constantly growing, but this is sufficient to indicate the serious and widespread interest in the test.

One of the most recent uses of the Ravich Interpersonal Game/ Test has been with the Marriage License Bureau of New York City. Here couples applying for a marriage license are asked to volunteer for a long-term research project that will analyze the couple's interaction before marriage and at regular intervals after the marriage in order to provide a more extensive observation and a further refinement of data on patterns of pair interaction. See also Appendix note 3.

the uninitiated it resembles an overgrown board game more than a test.[2] Nevertheless, it is an extraordinarily sophisticated information-gathering device that diagnoses the weaknesses, stresses, and strengths in the secret, innermost structure of a marriage or other pair relationship. It analyzes the human atom as accurately and dispassionately as ever a cloud chamber or a spectrophotometer analyzed the structure of beryllium. The way a pair plays this electric Train Game reflects exactly what is going on between them, how they solve conflicts, make decisions, cooperate, compete, domineer, submit, isolate themselves, or split.[3]

During the sixty or so minutes it takes to play the Train Game, a couple will reveal as much about themselves and their marriage as I or any other therapist could have discovered in six to twelve months of treatment. They replay their whole married life in that hour, and within fifteen minutes after they have completed the game I have a computer readout in front of me that reflects the marriage.* I liken the computer results to the streak of a falling star that flashed through the sky and disappeared centuries before its light became visible to our eyes. The computer printout is the trace of that falling star, a glimpse of the past in the present. It gives me a picture of the whole relationship—whether it covers twenty years or twenty months.

I will not know any details of their marital disagreements, their misunderstandings, their frustrations, but I

---

*When I use the term "marriage" here, it includes any ongoing, loving commitment of two people to each other, whether their union has been sanctioned by church or city hall or other official institution —or simply by themselves.

will have what is far more important than details—the *essence*, i.e., the essential structure, of the relationship. This essence is what most therapists try to synthesize from their painstaking hour-after-hour, month-after-month sessions during which the patients slowly use the details of their reactions to specific episodes as building blocks or brushstrokes in the process of constructing a picture of the total relationship. With the Train Game I have the essence of that relationship within an hour or two. And—another important factor—there is no danger that any of my personal feelings or reactions will have intruded to color or distort the picture of the relationship. The Train Game graph is as pure a picture of what goes on between two people as it is possible to obtain.

My testing of patients in private practice and at Cornell Medical College, at hospitals and clinics, as well as similar testing by my associates and by colleagues at the institutions I have listed, revealed that each marriage has an identifiable structure and a predictable pattern. And the dynamics of these marital structures make it clear for the first time why some marriages seem blessed, why others are destined to fail regardless of the love and respect each partner may have for the other and why certain other unions will never dissolve until death splits the human atom.

The findings of two independent research studies using the Train Game and involving 160 couples who were quite clearly "happily enough" married, and not in any kind of therapy, unmistakably indicated, in my opinion, that under most circumstances the patterns of interaction and the frequency of their presence are very similar to those of couples in therapy for serious marital discord, although some differences do become apparent when some type of stress is introduced into the situation. (The earlier stress study, by Michael Rothenberg, was a doctoral dissertation in clinical psychology done at Columbia University; the larger study was carried out by Dr. Bernard Liebowitz and his associates at Loyola University in Chicago, under a grant from the Illinois State Department of Mental Health to the Family Institute of Chicago.)

Up to now, those psychiatrists, psychologists, family counselors, and other professionals who are commonly consulted, at least by the affluent, when a marriage begins sending distress signals have themselves been flying by the seat of their pants, relying entirely upon intuition and experience as they tinkered with the ailing union, trying this palliative, then that, as they advised one partner or both to embark on a program of psychoanalysis, behavior modification, sexual experimentation, verbal hostilities to vent grievances, sensitivity training, hypnosis, or whatever. It was like trying to reach the moon in a Piper Cub. The intention might be laudable, but the means were certainly inadequate. Sometimes the marriage mechanics succeeded and sometimes they did not. I venture to say, in view of my findings, that they would have racked up an equal score of successes and failures if they had done nothing except send out their bills.

I am not impugning their intentions—or their integrity. They do the best they can; it is simply that I now know there is no way to hold some marriages together, even if the participants in these fated unions insist that they want their marriages to work—and mean it. This finding opens an entirely new field of practice to the helping professions—*marriage protection.* It is possible to spot with almost total accuracy which couples applying for marriage licenses will most probably hit the rocks of destructive strife and eventually wind up in the divorce court, just as I have been able to predict—simply by studying the computer printout of their interaction pattern as plotted by the Train Game—which couples who come to me for marital therapy will divorce.

The Train Game also makes it possible to identify those couples who are so tightly linked that they cannot, will not separate. These virtually indissoluble unions—and they include far more happy than unhappy marriages—represent the most common marital structure and may be the most important brake on our runaway divorce rate at the present time. When the marriage therapists enter the still practically nonexistent field of marriage protection, I think this will offer yet another, possibly even more effective brake to the divorce rate. For the first time, couples bent on matrimony will be able to weigh the predicted length and quality of the union against their needs and desires. This should act as a deterrent to many marriages that should never take place.

(When I think of the marriages that fall in this last category—virtually indissoluble but doomed to unhappiness—and when I think of what I would have liked to tell the men and women trapped in these unions if I had been able to counsel them before marriage, I ask myself if I am trying to play God. But the answer is No, an emphatic No. What I am trying to do when I counsel couples, after having established their interactive pattern through the Train Game, is to provide them with a kind of road map indicating the course of their union. If they don't like the route, they should think, think twice, thrice, a thousand times, before embarking on it.)

Between the extremes of marriages that are bound to fail and those that truly are until death does them part are marriages that can and should be strengthened. This is within the realm of possibility now that we can, so to speak, X-ray an individual union and pinpoint its strengths and weaknesses. Here is where the trained professional can intervene constructively and help couples rebuild their marriages into more comfortable, more rewarding environments.

I should make clear that this is no "how-to" book. It will not set an ailing marriage or relationship to rights. I look on it as a guide for both laymen and professionals to an unchartered territory—marriage. An institution as old as civilization, marriage has never before been subjected to scientific study. Remarkable as this may sound, we have never known what was going on inside this human atom, because the instruments to observe it, to measure it, were not available until recently.

Now we have the Train Game. When I discuss it with my colleagues or write about it in professional journals, I call it the RIG/T (Ravich Interpersonal Game/Test), but my patients and many of my colleagues have always referred to it as the Train Game. In this book, I accept their rule.[4]

2

Predicting Human Behavior

Recognizing patterns of interaction is just the first step on the long but hopeful road toward human predictability. And the very idea of accurate prediction of human behavior in this day when Big Brother is more than a fictive shadow frightens many people.

Is the Train Game really the key to a modern-day Pandora's box? Does it open the way to the last invasion of privacy? Will our interactive patterns be filed with the FBI or some superagency along with our fingerprints and our Social Security numbers? Will the predictability of interactive patterns lead to the control of the many by the few, puppets manipulable on the basis of inescapable behavior patterns?

It is understandable that these questions are raised. The age of innocence is over. Faith in government has been replaced by a cynical suspicion of all big organizations, including the bureaucracy in Washington, which has shown itself capable of being used to the advantage of those in high places (no matter how temporarily); the multiconglomerate business establishment, which transcends national boundaries and national interests for corporate profits; even the educational system, which has shown more interest in budgets than in the education of the young; and organized religion, which now seems to exist for the sake of existing. The result has been that the last stronghold of integrity and personal strength is the family, and particularly the nuclear pair at the core of each family. Even now, that core is under attack—economically, socially, culturally, intellectually, emotionally. And yet, if we are to correct and contain the excesses of anonymous macrobureaucracies, we must rely on this unit, the human atom.

I am convinced that the categorizing of patterns, the ability to predict interaction within the human dyad, will only lead to liberation, not regimentation or control. Patterns, once recognized, are nothing more or less than clues to the interaction between two individuals who form a nuclear pair. And that interactive pattern is unique. Within every dyad, there exists the possibility of sixty-four different kinds of interaction.[5] And each of the sixty-four exhibits some idiosyncratic twist that sets it aside from the interaction of another dyad with the same pattern. This means that individuals are not subject to interactive pigeonholing, because it takes two to interact and each dyad has its own distinctive interaction.

But if patterns then are so unique in their manifestations, how can I claim that human interactions are predictable? No matter how unique the circumstances, it is possible to predict with absolute accuracy that a Competitive pair (see page 55) will vie with each other, that a Cooperative pair (see page 55) will support each other's endeavors, and that a Dominant-Submissive pair (see page 53 for definition) will be long-lived, with a leader and a follower experiencing varying degrees of satisfaction in one of the strongest human relationships that exist. These elements can be predicted. We can forecast nuclear pairs that will have a calm or stormy relationship, a rewarding or destructive one, a long or short one, an exciting or boring one.

The following pages outline a case in which divorce was inevitable—and I knew it within two hours of meeting the couple for the first time. This is followed by a case of another couple for whom the Train Game opened a new route to compatibility.

3

Destination: Divorce

Julie and Jim played the Train Game in a distinctive, unmistakable manner. When I saw their graph, I shook my head. This couple was destined for divorce—and I had not been able to detect it from anything I had learned in my initial interview with them.

They had been very distressed. But all couples who seek marital therapy are distressed. They seemed quite obviously fond of each other and comfortable together, despite their problems. On the basis of our first meeting it would have been natural to expect that therapy would be brief—and effective. It was both of these, but the end result was not reconciliation but divorce.

There is one Train Game prediction that I have known to be wrong only once.* The Train Game can spot a certain category of divorce-bound couples immediately. There is no magic involved. It is simply that the interaction required and reflected by the game is an absolutely accurate diagnosis of what is really going on inside the nuclear couple. There are other couples with other patterns of interaction who divorce, but this is the only

*This exceptional case is described in Chapter 22.

category in which divorce seems just about inevitable.

Occasionally, a marriage that ends in divorce will cause me to think to myself, "If they had come to me earlier . . . if they had not allowed their problems to become so uncontrollable . . . if this . . . if that . . . this marriage could have been saved." But in the case of couples who play the Train Game the way Julie and Jim did, divorce appears to be almost inevitable. And therefore I do not consider it a failure when the couple start legal proceedings. Quite the contrary. I feel that I have helped by easing their separation, helping each partner to gain the strength to start afresh without any stigma of individual failure.

I want to stress that this is no instance of a self-fulfilling prophecy. I work as hard to help these couples as I do to help husbands and wives who have a better chance of making it together. Only after the divorce-prone couple itself acknowledges the impossibility of continuing as an intimate entity do I switch some of the emphasis of my therapy. Until that point, with each couple that comes to me exhibiting this special pattern and its several variations, I exercise my utmost inventiveness, experience, and dedication in treating them. But it does not lead to their staying married.

Julie and Jim were intelligent, very articulate people. And when Julie told me, after several months of treatment, that she had been keeping a kind of therapy diary, writing about her feelings and self-discoveries, I was, of course, interested. She showed me several entries, one of them about her reaction to the Train Game. It was a dramatic description of the game's immediate impact upon a player. It also hinted at the vast no-man's-land of indifference that had grown and was growing between husband and wife (and which the game had clearly delineated). With Julie's permission, I am using a slightly edited excerpt from her "therapy diary."

"The tester," Julie wrote, "cordial and courteous enough, was reserved to the point where spontaneity was stifled. She did not respond to any of the politely foolish remarks Jim and I made. She indicated that we were to sit at a small game table. I discovered later that this was purposeful. All interaction was to be confined to Jim and me. Her reserve was designed to keep the emotional atmosphere antiseptic. Something like an operating room.

"My first nervous impression was of a kind of spaghetti tangle of toy railroad tracks in front of me. I supposed Jim's side of the table was the same. I hadn't looked before I sat down, and now there was a panel between us, low enough so we could see each other, high enough to block our view of each other's tracks. With a second look, the tangle became simple enough. There was a starting point and almost immediately the first stretch of track forked; one fork led almost directly to the finish, the other looped about before reaching the end.

"The tester disappeared behind a partition and turned on a tape recording of her precise, passionless voice with instructions for playing the Train Game.* I resented her

---

*"Here are the instructions. Listen carefully. They cannot be repeated.

"Each person runs a train that must travel to the other end of the table. You gain or lose an imaginary penny for each second under or over thirty seconds that it takes you to get to your destination. Both can gain or both can lose, or one can gain and the other can lose.

"The layout of the tracks is the same for both, except that the engines start at opposite ends of the table. A short distance from the start there is a switch track that leads to either the Direct, straight route or the Alternate, winding route. If you both take the Direct

detachment. It made me feel that Jim and I were really alone in that room. And I didn't like that. Why did we have to be in some sort of isolation ward just because we were driving each other crazy? I tried to concentrate on the instructions, but from the very beginning I had trouble in absorbing them. Almost the first statement was the fact that the tester could not answer any questions. That got me upset. There was so much to take in.

"Later Dr. Ravich told us that the instructions contained fifty items of information. No wonder I panicked.* But at the moment I was desperately trying to

---

Route, you can collide. If a collision occurs, the engines stop moving and a red light on your control panel flashes on and off. Then, one or the other or both of you have to back up—or you can both stand still head-on. Also, on the other person's Direct Route you control a barrier which can block the other person's train—and the other person can block yours. The barriers are open at the start of each trip. They can be closed and opened any time during a trip. A red light alongside your Direct track means you've been blocked by the other person.

"On the Alternate Route, there are no collisions and no barriers.

"There will be a number of trips. On each trip a green light on your control panel tells you to start. The red light tells you to press either the Direct or Alternate button. The black lever will move your train to forward, stop, or reverse. If you want to change route, bring your train all the way back to start and press the other button. The other two buttons can open or close the barrier on the other person's side.

"The total running times and profit or loss will be displayed by the score box after each trip when I return the trains to their start position. You can talk to each other as much as you want.

"This is the end of the instructions.

"We will begin the first trip shortly."

*Julie's intense reaction is shared by a certain number of individuals, but the fact is that some four-year-old children receiving the very same instructions have no difficulty understanding them and playing the Train Game. So did Julie and Jim. It is important to realize that

make sense of all the information being thrown at us. At the same time I was worrying about what this game was going to do to our marriage. Jim was sitting there, half angry, half sullen. I was afraid he would get up and walk out.

"The instructions for the game seemed interminable. At one point I was confused when the taped voice said that if we both took the Direct Route, our trains would collide. I couldn't understand how Jim's train or mine could leap over the screen and collide. Later on, I asked Dr. Ravich if I could read the instructions. I discovered that my question had been answered in the very next sentence, but I completely missed it at the time.

"Finally the instruction tape came to an end. The tester took over. I could tell the difference, the real voice from the taped voice.

" 'The first trip will begin when the green light goes on,' she said.

" 'What will we do?' I asked.

" 'I don't know,' Jim said. 'I'm not good at games.' I knew he was giving up already. Whatever went on would not be his fault, because he was refusing to take it seriously. He was right, of course. He was lousy at games.* He didn't play them. He had never joined me and the children in any of those endless games of Parcheesi and

---

there is no real winning or losing in the Train Game. In the words of the idealists, "It's how you play that matters."

*Since life itself is a "game" in a sense, the person who does not like to play games, who avoids games, may be playing a game of his own, a game he tries to win (or lose) by refusing to participate. This is also shown up in the Train Game. In Jim's case, it was very evident —he limited his participation, going his own way at his own pace, and refusing any interaction with his wife.

Monopoly and Chinese Checkers and Scrabble that seem
to be part of growing up.

" 'We have to do something,' I said. 'We can't just sit
here.'

" 'I don't see why not,' Jim said flatly. But he evidently
flicked his switch and took the Direct Route. I had done
the same thing. And we had a collision. Suddenly I understood about that common stretch of track. We each
had separate tracks, but they were electrically connected
so that when our trains, moving in opposite directions,
meet, there is a simulated electronic collision. Both
trains stopped. I waited.

" 'I'm not going to back up,' Jim announced gleefully.

"I shrugged my shoulders. Winning this stupid game
didn't mean anything to me. I thought it was ridiculous
of Dr. Ravich to think that people like Jim and me were
going to put our hearts into a game just to win a few
theoretical cents. I didn't care if I lost. So I backed all the
way to the starting point, then flicked the switch and
went off again, this time on the Alternate Route, where
I went up hill and down dale (that's what it seemed like)
forever (and that's what it seemed like, too, although it
was less than a minute). Jim finished long before me.

"That passionless voice announced, 'Jim won seven
cents on trip one. Julie lost forty-two cents.' So? Who
cares?

"Then came trip two. And trip three. I kept taking the
Alternate Route. It was kind of fun watching the train
make its way around the curves. But not for long. Actually it was dull, dull, dull. I was almost out of my skin with
boredom. However, I didn't have to get into any hassle
with Jim about collisions. He was bad-tempered enough
about having the psychiatrist of his choice turn out to be

some kook who made him play games without my forcing him to any confrontations in the game. I was still scared he might walk out—just the way he had walked out on the psychiatrist of my choice, whom we'd seen a couple of weeks earlier.

"Trip nine. I was still losing; he was still winning. We both were mighty bored. But trip ten will be the end, I reassured myself. This little trial by boredom will soon be over.

"Dear God! 'Trip eleven will start when the green light goes on.'

"Could there be another *five* of these? Fifteen trips in all? Each of those Alternate Route trips seemed a lifetime and a half. What about something different?

"I thought of a way I could stop being the big loser— a way we could come out even.

" 'Jim, look, let's take turns. Instead of you taking the Direct Route all the time, take the Alternate this time and I'll take the Direct. Then next trip, we'll switch. OK?'

"Jim agreed. And it worked.

"Finally! The fifteenth trip.

"Inexorably, the voice came from behind the partition, 'Trip sixteen will start when the green light goes on.'

"We looked at each other. Raised our eyebrows. Perhaps the test was designed to test the limits of endurance. Well, we were both the type to stick with it, no matter what.

"So it went trip after trip after trip. Jim won. I lost. Then I won and Jim lost. Back and forth we went, switching routes each time. Oh, and I forgot the Chinese water torture. As soon as the green light begins for each trip, the beeping begins. A loud beep like the alarm clock in your nightmare. Beep beep beep beep. A beep a second.

Thirty, forty, sixty beeps to a trip. Sometimes more.
Every second we were conscious of boring time passing.
Would we ever finish?

"Finally! This had to be it. The twentieth game. No.
There was that voice announcing the beginning of another trip.* Some trip!

"Jim was getting more sullen as he got more bored,
but we both tried to converse in our best company manner. Actually we were fairly well-disposed toward each
other today. We had this worthy feeling that we were
doing the right thing, taking a constructive step. Somehow, without saying it to each other, we wanted to convince this psychiatrist that we got along well together.
Crazy! I wondered how Jim thought I felt about the
whole thing. He probably didn't even spend one of those
long ticked-off seconds wondering about how I felt or
what I thought.

"The twenty-fifth trip. And the twenty-sixth. I felt the
way I had as a little girl when my mother ripped out my
lumpy knitting because I had made so many mistakes and
told me to start all over again. My head hurt. I felt like
throwing up. And I knew it wouldn't do any good. You
just had to get on with it.

"I wondered if the secret of the game was seeing who
would give up and walk out first. If that was the secret,
why didn't I do it half an hour ago?

"What? The end? Twenty-eight trips? That's an odd
number. Four times seven. Is there any significance in
that? Anyway, ours was not to reason why; ours was but
to do and die of boredom. How to smother a marriage
before lunch."

*The number of trips in a session is variable. For the sake of
simplicity, twenty trips are given in this book for an average session.

Julie's impressionistic but quite faithful description of the way she and Jim played the game was a better reflection of their pattern of interaction than the tape of their comments as they played, for their conversation, while it reflected some impatience and resentment, was consciously innocuous. When I looked at Julie's and Jim's graph, I recognized their chatter for the window dressing it was. Here was the truth: they were going to divorce. It always made me sad to see this pattern emerge.

Julie and Jim had played out a very significant pattern, one that shows up in about 1 percent of the cases I see. I call it the Divorce Route, because, on the surface, it seems very cooperative and amicable, yet—as I said—this pattern indicates divorce.

This conclusion will become self-explanatory when I discuss Julie's and Jim's case in more detail in Chapter 21. In any event, this is a marriage that could have been prevented if the Train Game had been available during their courtship. Any therapist who has been trained in my technique of analyzing graphs would have spotted their abortive pattern immediately. The breakup of this marriage was utterly predictable.

This raises another question: *Should* this marriage have been prevented? I'm not so sure of the answer. For Julie and Jim, I believe the marriage was an enriching experience, that each contributed to the growth of the other. But divorce—inevitable or not—is always a trauma. It takes a sturdy personality to sail through these stormy waters to . . . and that is another question, what lies beyond? It is a terra incognita. Even the Train Game cannot predict the future. My researches in this area are only just now getting underway. It will take at least a decade before we have enough solid information to venture definitive answers. But in the meantime, my visceral feeling is that, yes, some of these marriages are worth-while—if the partners are strong enough to handle the inevitable dissolution. And it's important to recognize that no nuclear couple is ever completely dissolved. There is always some interaction between the partners, sometimes stronger, sometimes weaker, but always there.

Even after divorce, even when no children are in-volved, there is an emotional tie, an electric connection, between former partners that never completely disap-pears. It may fade and weaken to an occasional fleeting memory—sour or sweet. It may take the form of a spon-taneous, "Oh, John [or Jane] would have liked this . . . or hated that," or "I wish he/she could see how well I'm doing without him/her." But some divorced couples succeed in maintaining a somewhat distant but pleasant and constructive relationship based on the knowledge and appreciation they have gained of each other's strengths and weaknesses. Those who achieve this can reassure themselves that their married years were not wasted years, but a time of mutual growth.

4

Destination: Compatibility

One of my most successful (and most satisfying) cases demonstrated that the Train Game is so absolutely basic that it even transcends language. Among the first players of the game in its initial version, when it was a Ping-Pong-sized layout, were a Puerto Rican couple who spoke no English.

The Delgados were the first non–English-speaking pair to play the Train Game. The interpreter read the instructions in Spanish, and they started playing with its two trains. They did not say a word to each other as each directed his or her own train in trip after trip. Julio Delgado always took the Direct Route to the end of the line. Donna avoided all confrontations or collisions by choosing the Alternate Route each time. It was an absolutely undeviating Dominant-Submissive pattern. He was barreling ahead without heed; she acceded.

In those days, I did not have instant computer feedback after a game, so the postgame sessions were held a week later. As the Delgados walked in the following week, their faces fell. They were obviously disappointed about something. They explained to the interpreter that they had been talking about the game all week and were looking forward to playing it again. But where was it? It had disappeared.

The game took up so much room that I only had it set up when a new couple was coming in for diagnosis. But when the interpreter explained to me that Donna and Julio had been talking about the game all week, I got to work and set it up for them. I had learned in our pregame interview that the couple had a most severe communication problem. In fact, they rarely spoke to each other at all. Days would go by without their exchanging more than a word or two. Now, suddenly, they had begun to talk. Some barrier between them had fallen and they had found a subject that they wanted to talk about. This was sufficient reason to set up the game again.

The Delgados sat down contentedly at the testing table and played—just exactly the same way as they had the week before. She took the long Alternate Route, he took the short Direct one. With the aid of the interpreter, I interrupted then and started coaching, saying, "Now, you have to talk to each other. You have to tell each other what you are doing. That way, you can each come out ahead." But they wouldn't. Or they couldn't.

This went on for weeks. Their therapy consisted of the Train Game. Each week I would tell them through the interpreter that they had to talk to each other. If they did, I assured them, they would work out a way for both of them to win, not just Julio. But it did not seem to get through to them.

Finally, weeks after their first visit, the Delgados did begin to talk to each other, to tell each other what they were doing on their sides of the panel and to work out an arrangement by which both could win. Their discussions, as relayed to me by the interpreter, were fascinating and touching. Donna said that she would not take the

Direct Route, because she knew that Julio would be on that route and she did not want to collide with him. Besides that, she said, "I used to like seeing the trains wind around the mountains in Puerto Rico. Now I pretend that I am on a train and I am winding around in those mountains and those green valleys."

Like many Dominant-Submissives, Julio and Donna were depressed. Donna had become obese. She would often cry, but could never tell Julio what she was crying about. And he was a very agitated, very scared man. He worked as a presser; the work was hard, the hours long, and the pay poor. He worried that they would fire him because he was getting old. He could not speak English so he felt alienated from the world around him. On top of that, he felt alienated from Donna, because he never knew what was going on with her. He could never understand why she cried.

All this was reflected in the way they played the game. As they progressed and started talking to each other, they worked out an interesting mode of play. When it was Donna's agreed-upon turn to come out second, she would wait until there was no risk of colliding with Julio on the Direct Route before she started out. Julio, on the other hand, would eagerly go ahead when it was his turn to be second and crash into Donna. He would back up immediately. It was simply a sign of how much he desired to be in touch with her. In just a matter of weeks, they had shifted from a Dominant-Submissive pattern to a Cooperative pattern.* At the same time, their conversation grew richer. They started talking about the children, about going shopping, about Julio's job.

One day, they came in and excitedly told the story of

*See page 55.

their weekend. In the summer, they always went to the park with the children on Sundays. Donna would bring sausages and fruit and they would stop at a bakery and buy two loaves of bread—a big round family-sized loaf and a long French loaf. When they got to the park, Donna would sit on a bench and watch the children race around. When they got hungry, she would portion out the round loaf of bread and unpack the rest of the lunch. Julio always sat on the grass under a tree about thirty feet away from the family. He would drink his beer, eat his sausage with chunks from the long French loaf. There was no contact between Julio and Donna.

But this last Sunday, when they had stopped at the bakery, they had bought only one loaf of bread, a big round one. And Julio had joined his wife on the bench instead of retreating to his spot under the tree. The whole family had picnicked together for the first time.

They were truly excited, exclaiming that "It's like the game! We used to take separate tracks, now we take the same one!" They understood the symbolism of the game as well as any more sophisticated couple.

This breakthrough was accompanied by other changes. Donna had been losing weight. She had also started to learn English, going to a class at the settlement house. Julio was still nervous, overworked, and worried about keeping his job, but he had calmed down considerably now that he felt in touch with his wife once more. Learning about themselves through the Train Game had helped them help themselves.

5

The Dying Game

Before I outline the patterns of marital (and extramarital) interaction revealed by the Train Game and the joys, heartbreak, tedium, hysteria, contentment, excitement, disappointment, rivalry, fulfillment, and expectations inherent in these patterns, I think it will be helpful to the reader to know a little about the evolution of the Train Game and to understand some of the philosophic principles behind it in order to accept the concept that the interactions elicited by the game can truly blueprint the intimate relationship between two people.

Those who prefer to plunge ahead should turn now to Chapter 8: "The Big Three, the Minor Four, and the Chaotic Eighth," in which I embark on a description of the various patterns of interaction. For those who want to proceed logically, step by step, with facts more or less in hand, this chapter and the two following it (along with the appendix references) constitute a brief history of the development of my thinking about the secret game that exists between every pair of lovers, every husband and wife, in every intimate dyadic relationship. And this microhistory, by its very nature, contains a capsule review of the development of the Train Game.

To understand the genesis of the Train Game, one must realize that in the history of ideas, there are very few that spring full-blown from the mind like Botticelli's Venus from the scallop shell. Einstein did not wake up one morning and exclaim, "Eureka! I have discovered relativity!"

Flashes of insight do lead to breakthroughs great and small, and at the moment the discovery may seem the purest instant serendipity to outsiders. But in historical fact it is usually the distillation of the discoverer's life experience, the researches and ideas of others, often an advance in technology that opens new possibilities, and, finally, his own logic and intuition that result in the breakthrough.

And so it was with the development of this diagnostic test, the Train Game, which enables us to understand the structure of the interaction between any two people and particularly that between husband and wife. My own background, the researches of others, the new computer technology, an ancient book of learning (see Appendix note 5, page 248)—all were synthesized in the development of the Train Game over a period of years. And the game itself was the unique, new tool, itself an advance in technology, that enabled me to analyze and calibrate the structure of the human atom, the nuclear couple that is the basis of our civilization.

So I hope I will be forgiven an excursion into personal history.

Like many young men, I was greatly influenced by my father in the choice of a career. He was a urologist engaged in cancer research. I, too, became a physician. And when I returned to civilian life after World War II, I joined my father in cancer research. With two other colleagues, we formed the Institute of Applied Biology, a foundation-funded research organization, and within a few years we had our own hospital on the Upper East Side of Manhattan (we called it Trafalgar Hospital after its telephone exchange) where we worked to develop biochemical methods of controlling cancer.

Apart from the excitement and hope integral in almost any scientific study, this was a grueling, heart-rending undertaking. In the first place, all of the Institute's patients were judged to be beyond help from any surgical or radiological procedures when they were referred to us. Death and anxiety were in the very air we breathed. And those of us involved in research customarily worked seven-day weeks. Death observed no weekends—and neither did we. There was little respite for any of the staff from the compounded horror of death after death after death.

My particular responsibility was to get the medical history and make a complete, initial physical examination of each patient. My task was complicated by the fact that at the very least, three out of four of these men and women with advanced malignancies had never been told the true nature of their illness. Neither their physicians nor their families had ever said "cancer" to them. Nor did most of our patients seem (or wish) to realize that they were part of a cancer research project. And there were excellent reasons why we did not tell them but went along with the system that then prevailed in work with terminal cancer patients.[6]

A protective structure of lies and distortions had been erected around these dying men and women. This structure seemed to be of vital importance—not so much to the patients but to their families. A pattern that I had

been conscious of from my earliest days as an intern
unfolded afresh and even more strikingly, starting with
the very first patient I ever admitted to the research
program.

Mr. A. had been referred to us by a distinguished
surgeon. A "hopeless" cancer case, the doctor had said.
His body was eaten up with the spreading malignancy. It
was raging through his system. It was a matter of two
weeks, two days, a month perhaps. It was impossible to
tell.

The day before Mr. A. was to be admitted, his brother
telephoned. He had to see me, he said, to talk to me
before his brother came to the hospital. I was very busy
and suggested that he wait until I had examined his
brother. I would be better equipped to discuss the case
then. No. That would not do. He had to see me. That
very day. I agreed.

He was in my office an hour later. The essence of what
he had to say was that his brother, Mr. A., did not know
he had cancer, much less that he was dying. His doctor
had not told him. Neither had his family.

"How could this be?" I asked in amazement.

"Oh, there was no problem," the brother said. "When
he had his first operation, the doctor simply told him that
he had removed a benign polyp." The surgeon had not
mentioned seeing the swollen, stiffened tissue surround-
ing it and other telltale signs of cancer. After Mr. A. had
undergone more surgery a few months later, the surgeon
told him that part of his intestine had been removed, that
an ulcerous section had been excised. And so it had
gone.

I nodded. And I agreed that I would not tell Mr. A. that

he had cancer. I was a young physician. Mr. A. had been under the care of older, more experienced men whom I respected. And these physicians had not only set up this conspiratorial situation but had suggested that the family go along with this "loving lie." I was disturbed, but I felt I had no choice.

After a dozen more such interviews with relatives of patients, I recognized that this "game" was almost universal and that no one seemed to find it difficult or impossible to play it, not relatives, not doctors, not nurses —and, as I discovered, not even the patients themselves. It seemed to be second nature.

I was continually impressed with the technique of one of our most competent nurses at Trafalgar. When she first came into a new patient's room, she would routinely ask what was wrong with him. And whatever he told her —arthritis, inflamed gall bladder, ulcers, whatever—she would enter on his chart. From then on, as far as the staff was concerned, that was the name of that patient's disease.

I discovered that I could eliminate most preadmittance family conferences by asking at the time of referral if the patient knew what his illness was. I was usually informed that he did not. Then when that inevitable telephone call from the relative came, I would assure him or her, right then and there, that I understood the patient did not know he had cancer—and that we would not tell him. This assurance was usually sufficient.

Within a few months, I made another discovery. *At least half (and probably more) of the patients who supposedly did not know they had cancer knew it very well.* They knew exactly what was wrong with them. When I was able to pick this up from various hints they dropped,* I would give them an opening to talk about it. Some ignored the opening, but others seized on it avidly. It was clear that they found great relief in being able to talk about cancer, about death.

The dying man or woman who finally was able to talk about his disease with me or with other staff members usually kept up the pretense with friends and family. Their rationale? They wanted to "protect" their wives and husbands, their children, their friends from the fearful facts. Just as their families tried to protect them. And they wanted me to cooperate with them in this pretense.

This made me sad—sometimes angry, often outraged, but always sad. I felt that the game was being carried to an unnecessary extreme. It denied the patients the open expressions of love and support and understanding that could have added emotional ease and comfort to their last days. By contrast, in the handful of cases I observed where family and patient were finally able to acknowledge the truth and talk about it, the sense of relief was tremendous. The tension was diminished. The lonely burden had been lifted. There were more tears, but there was also more warmth, more empathy. The barriers were down. Communication flowed. This was the last closeness.

But most patients resisted. I asked one woman if she had told her family that she knew. "No," she said pain-

---

*I remember one man with lung cancer who had quite obviously read up on lung diseases. He discoursed knowledgeably on emphysema, atelectasis, bronchiectasis, pneumonitis, tuberculosis, silicosis. But he never mentioned cancer, a direct giveaway to the subject uppermost on his mind.

fully. "It would make it too hard for them. It's better they think I have hope."

Why could some people acknowledge death—not only to themselves, but to those whom they loved and who loved them? And why could others never admit it? What was this game all about? And what was the signal that allowed the rule of silence to be broken? What was it that took place in those cases where the living and the dying were finally able to break the taboo and acknowledge the truth?

As the years passed, I became convinced that in almost *every* case, not just the majority, both participants, the healthy and the dying, knew. The dying knew that they had cancer and would die. And the living knew that the dying knew. I believed that they were grateful to the dying for permitting them to play out this grim charade of ignorance. To most, dying was the ultimate obscenity. And the living could not face it. So the rules between this dyad, the living and the dying, were set up to ease the transition—ease it for the living. And the rules were as rigid as those of a child's going-to-bed ritual.

I eventually stopped thinking of this pretense and counterpretense as a game. I accepted it as the way things were. It was life—and death. The rules were the defenses of the spirit. They formed a shield that in some cases allowed the individual to come to terms with mortality at his own pace, and in other cases locked him into a self-imposed deception.

It was almost as hard for me as it was for any patient or relative. The detachment that the medical profession is thought to cultivate is hard won. I could hardly maintain it. I often cried when we lost a patient—and most of our patients were terminal when they came to us. Even when a course of treatment seemed to be working, when the malignant advance was halted, at least for a while, few of these men and women had enough stamina left to maintain life. I admired them. They fought so hard. The disease was an agony and so, most often, was the treatment. Yet, they maintained a dignity. There was a triumph in the way many met death. A triumph that I could not share—because I had failed. The symptoms of my failure were insomnia, diarrhea, nervous stomach, tension. There is a gnawing anguish in watching people die, knowing that you cannot help them.

There came a day when I thought it was not only unfair to myself, but to my family as well, to go on this way. Even when I was home, my heart and mind were half in the hospital. I took a weekend off, a golden October weekend. My wife and I visited friends who had a house on the Jersey shore. We walked miles along the beach. The Atlantic was as blue as the October sky. Everything was salt-clean, windswept. Death, illness, hospitals seemed far away. Yes, it was time to make a break. There was more to life.

But yet, how could I give up this research now? Every month we hoped for a breakthrough. Every month we were disappointed, but in a way I was like a compulsive gambler. I wouldn't, couldn't give it up. Perhaps next month we would find a cure. Or the next. We had had some promising results. But in the meantime, how could I continue to sign three and four death certificates a week? The strain was too much now.

Nevertheless, I decided to stick with it. I would make a conscious effort to be less involved. I would force myself to accept the inevitable, to armor myself against it. Less empathy, more professionalism. I would play the game.

It is easier to *decide* not to feel than it is to stop feeling. But that archetypal game between the living and the dying helped. I was able to deny the inevitable. Until I faced another death.

I used to dream about the hospital. And in my dreams, everyone wore a mask. They were the traditional theater masks of tragedy and comedy. I was becoming more and more obsessed with the idea that life was one huge game and that the final interplay between the living and the dying was just one phase of this game. But what were the rules? If it was a game.[7]

Whatever it was, the ritual of the game did help. But denial had its limits. And after ten years, I finally decided that I had had enough—I wanted to go into psychiatry, and I did.

6

Secret Marital Games

My original plan when I entered psychiatry was to return eventually to cancer research. For some time I had suspected that the development and course, if not the actual cause, of certain malignant tumors had a psychological or emotional basis. I also wanted to explore the psychiatric aspects of chronic physical illness. A solid psychiatric background was necessary to pursue these researches.

But immediately and acutely I became aware of elaborate games being played out by the patients and the staff members in the New York State Psychiatric Institute, where I was an assistant resident, just as patients, family, and staff had engaged in games at Trafalgar Hospital. And the rules in these games, although here they were rarely life-and-death games, were equally, almost primitively, compelling, as urgent as hunger and thirst and sex. This was especially true of the unformulated rules that dominate below the level of consciousness, often contravening existing social rules and transcending the pseudo-realities of bureaucracy, administrative convenience, and theory systems.

One accepted rule, for instance, that governed psychiatric therapy at that period—and it was only fifteen years ago—was that the method was a one-to-one process—the doctor and the patient. The environment that had molded the patient was considered only at secondhand, through the patient's descriptions and reactions as assessed by the therapist.

But this rule was being increasingly breached by the irrepressible intrusion of reality. Its rigidity was under attack in our hospital by the late Dr. Nathan W. Ackerman, who at that time was an attending psychiatrist at New York State Psychiatric Institute and a professor at the Columbia University Psychoanalytic Clinic, parts of the psychiatric teaching-and-treatment maze attached to the Columbia complex. A highly controversial figure then, Dr. Ackerman was a pioneer in family therapy. His idea that the whole family should be involved in the treatment, not just the individual who presented the symptoms, was considered an amusing notion by some, heresy by others, and a brilliant breakthrough by the more perceptive, open-minded men in the field. It was only because of his influence that I was able to flout the one-to-one "establishment" rule occasionally during my training.

In two instances, by disregarding the traditional one-to-one relationship, I was able not only to make significant progress in treating patients, but—and not merely incidentally—to change the direction of my professional career.

The first was the case of eleven-year-old Sally. Everyone at the clinic knew Sally or at least was familiar with her case, because the first of her numerous admittances had been at the age of four.* She had bounced from bad to better to worse over the years. Now she was extremely difficult to treat. She trusted no one. She always worried, "What are they saying about me?" She was particularly concerned about what I and other staff members said about her at the weekly conference.

This weighed so much on her mind that I suggested we allow her to attend a meeting, but this was too radical a procedure for the head of the department. I was given permission, however, to set up a mock mini-meeting consisting of Sally, the nurse in charge of the ward, and myself. Without saying a word about it, Sally asked a young medical student who was working on the ward to come to the meeting. When I saw him, it became clear to me that Sally had engineered a grouping that reflected her family. I was the father, the nurse her mother, and the young medical student represented her older brother, whom she admired. I was struck by this. Was she trying to tell me something? Should I bring her family into her treatment?

It was worth a try.

And indeed it was. Our meetings with Sally's family proved to be the turning point in her case. After one of these sessions, Sally's mother revealed that from the time Sally was eighteen months old until she was four, her parents had forcibly administered almost daily enemas. This key fact had never come out earlier—not

---

*Sally's case has been reported by Drs. L. S. Kubie and H. Israel in "Say You're Sorry," in *The Psychoanalytic Study of the Child*, Volume 10 (New York: International Universities Press, 1955); and by Drs. R. A. Ravich and H. D. Dunton in " 'Say You're Sorry!'—A Ten-Year Follow-up" in the *Amer. J. Psychotherapy*, 20, no. 4 (October 1966).

even the first time Sally was admitted to the clinic, at the age of four.

Even the case-hardened doctors in the clinic shuddered. It would be hard to devise a more effective way of warping a child's sense of bodily integrity, of competence, of trust. At the age when most parents start to toilet-train a child, Sally's parents had subjected her to painful, involuntary evacuations and had seen to it that she had no control over her body. The resultant psychic trauma had affected her sexually, emotionally, and intellectually.

Her parents *seemed* pleasant enough, intelligent enough, normal enough. Yet—what was this sadistic game? It was always the same. The father would hold down the wildly protesting child and her mother would squirt soapy water into her daughter's rectum. When they were asked why they did this, they had no explanation other than that they thought she was constipated and uncomfortable, even though the pediatrician had told them repeatedly that there was no reason to worry about Sally's bowel movements.

This case affected me profoundly. It was my first experience of the utter inevitability of what I was starting to think of as "reality rules," although at the time I believed that the meaningful breakthrough had been in seeing the total family constellation, not just one member. Added to that was the satisfaction that I was surprised to find in myself at recognizing that a game was being played by Sally's mother and father. A satisfaction that was not at all marred by the unanswered questions that nagged at me: How did they ever get the idea of this torture by enema? Why did the two of them continue with the enemas for such a long time? Did they ever discuss what they were doing? Question it? And then, how had they managed to conceal it for so long? What kind of conniv- ance was this? What were the rules of this marriage?

I needed to know more about what went on between people, particularly between husbands and wives.

The second case that proved to be a turning point in my life reinforced my perception, gained from the expe- rience with Sally, that there was something going on between husbands and wives that had not yet been de- tected, much less understood. But I was convinced that this "something" existed the way some people believe in God and others accept the fact that enormous galaxies wheel about in the universe at unimaginable distances.

I had been treating a member of the Columbia faculty, a fine man, very intelligent, who was seriously depressed. He had been hospitalized because of a suicide attempt, and now I was working with him, trying to help him cope with his depression. There was something holding up the treatment. I couldn't put my finger on it: some intan- gible barrier. After a few weeks I began to suspect that the "intangible" something was his very tangible wife. My patient dropped several hints that she did not ap- prove of his being in therapy, did not think he needed it, did not like the idea of his seeing me three times a week. I was puzzled by this, because I knew that she had been psychoanalyzed. It didn't make any sense—her resisting his having therapy.

One morning she called and announced that her hus- band could not keep his appointment that day. A family emergency had called him out of town. I suggested that she come in his place. I wanted to talk to her and ask some questions about her husband, about their relation- ship.

She came to the office and was very cooperative. I sensed none of the resistance that I had been led to believe existed. I was very surprised. She talked openly and even asked my advice on certain problems. The family emergency continued to disrupt my patient's routine for several weeks. He had to break three or four more appointments. Each time, his wife came in his place.

Finally I suggested to her, "Why don't you come *with* Calvin next time. After all, it now seems as if I'm treating you both, so why don't I treat you together?"

"Let me ask Calvin what he thinks," she replied. Her husband was obviously agreeable, because the two of them showed up together at the next session.

In the meantime, I had been scurrying about frantically to get permission from the Institute to see the two of them together. It sounds fairly commonplace today. But at that time conjoint marital therapy (treating both members of the couple together) was a revolutionary step. If it had not been for Dr. Ackerman's pioneering work, I doubt that I would have received permission.[8]

The joint session with husband and wife was a revelation. He was a different man, a suspicious tyrant. The way he acted when his wife was present bore no relation to his behavior when he was alone with me. It was like seeing another person. She, too, was somewhat different, but not to the same startling degree. (And it also turned out that she had never resisted her husband's having therapy. His hints to this effect had been part of a smokescreen he had used to obscure their relationship.)

It was like bringing the correct proportions of oxygen and hydrogen together and watching water being

formed in front of one's eyes. I could not have imagined
such a convincing demonstration that my suspicions
were true: Something existed between husbands and
wives, something significant in their joint behavior. It
was clear that these two people interacting with each
other were much different from either one of the two
alone with me—or with someone else. A completely different unit had emerged—the nuclear pair. And I had to
change my approach to the case almost completely. I was
no longer treating the husband or the wife or the husband *and* the wife, but a single entity, analogous to the
nucleus of the atom. This was the marital reality—the
couple.

I couldn't get over it. Suddenly I saw marital therapy
as a new and exciting frontier. No longer was it a matter
of trying to reconcile warring, straying, furious, or miserable couples. It was treating an entity, an entity that I had
not known existed. It was like discovering a new planet
or isolating a new element.

My psychiatric training was nearly over. The time was
coming when I would reenter private practice. And I
knew now where my real interest lay—not in the psychological aspects of malignancies and disease, but in exploring what really went on inside the marital unit.

What was the game? What were the rules?

7

Birth of a Game

When I returned to private practice, this time as a psychiatrist, I found myself increasingly bewildered by this entity, the nuclear couple. It proved to be very elusive. There were times when I thought of the couples sitting in my office as a handful of that children's plaything Silly Putty. Every time I had a firm grasp of their relationship, it would slip between my fingers, change its shape and elude me.

It was next to impossible, for instance, to explore the motivations of one partner in depth, because the other kept reacting, and usually vehemently, to every statement. Old conflicts surfaced faster than I could absorb them. The interaction within the couple was too fast. Accusations were hurled. There was shouting, there were tears. There was no time to probe the marital wounds. At times during a session with a warring couple, I would feel that I was on a runaway treadmill. By the end of the treatment hour I would be exhausted, not to mention frustrated, because I had not been able to slow the interaction down to the point where we could start examining the sources of their mutual problems. It was as if I were a spectator at a revved-up tennis game, my atten-

tion oscillating between the players so fast that everything was a blur.

The husband or wife would try to woo my support
against the other. Or they would insist that I adjudicate
their conflicts and hand out verdicts of guilty and not
guilty.

The most puzzling aspect of these cases was my feeling
that the couples were playing some sort of game with me
and with each other, a game they didn't want me to learn.
I found myself just as perplexed by the husbands and
wives who sought me out for marital therapy as I had
been by little Sally's parents. I could not figure out what
was going on with them.

On top of that, I was disappointed to find that my plan
to treat couples as a single unit, a kind of human atom,
did not seem to be feasible. The reality was that I was
seeing both husband and wife at the same time in the
same place—and treating each individually. I would try
to help one achieve some insight into his actions and
then the other. But I could have done this more efficiently by seeing the partners separately. I could not
seem to find a way to treat the couple as a couple, a unit.
There was so much emotional flak and so little constructive discussion at our joint sessions that I often despaired
of helping them learn to function effectively and live with
each other. I considered giving up conjoint therapy, but
still I kept hoping for some kind of breakthrough—just
as I had hoped during the cancer research.

"If only I could figure out what game they're playing,"
I would say to myself. "If only I could figure out the rules
they're using, I could break through all this." I was positive that they were playing a game and wanted to keep
me guessing. They didn't really want me to understand

their interactions. They were challenging me, I thought.

But as I gathered more experience, I changed my mind. I gradually became convinced that they did not know they were playing a game. And, instead of their trying to hide things from me, the truth was quite the contrary. Most patients tend to attribute God-like powers to their psychiatrist; these couples were confident that I knew exactly what was going on between them. And when the time was ripe, they were sure I would explain it all to them.

But I *didn't* know. It was like trying to put together a vast abstract jigsaw puzzle with a handful of pieces missing. I became haunted by the notion of games. Why did people play games? And what were these games? I had to find out.

I started by studying everything I could find on game theory. Game theory is a creation of abstract mathematics, but in its essentials it is not too much different from the old childhood game of holding both hands behind one's back and asking someone to guess which hand holds the candy or the penny.

The first guess is pure chance. The second guess— that's different. The one who chooses thinks, "Well, I chose the right hand last time and it was empty. This time he will expect me to choose the left hand. And so he will be holding the candy in his right hand. All right, I will choose the right hand again."

Then he hesitates. "But no. That's just what he thinks I will do. He thinks that I will have thought just what I have thought. And so he will not change. The candy will still be in the left hand. So I will choose the left hand. He can't fool me."

Depending on the youngster, he may or may not hesitate again and say to himself, "But no. That is just what he thinks I think he thinks I have thought. And he will outwit me. The candy will be in the right hand."

And so it may go back and forth, weaving ever more intricate suppositions of "he thinks that I think that he thinks that I think." But the choices still remain only the left hand or the right hand.

It is the rare youngster who introduces a third choice —neither hand—by surreptitiously slipping the candy or penny into a pocket. And it is the still rarer child who conceives that this may be the fact and chooses this unorthodox third solution.

Game theory as a modern concept stems from the effort during World War II to improve the accuracy of anti-aircraft guns and, at the same time, develop flying patterns that offered maximum protection from anti-aircraft fire. Mathematician John von Neumann was the pioneer in this field. Later, with economist Oskar Morgenstern, he applied his theories to economic forces and suggested that game theory be applied to other social sciences.[9]

Then I discovered that several social psychologists had been developing games as a means of studying people's reactions. The first significant game along these lines was Prisoner's Dilemma, a mainstay of elementary psychology courses, which has been extensively explored by Anatol Rapaport and his students. But the game that caught my imagination was called the Acme-Bolt Trucking Game. It was developed by Professor Morton Deutsch, a social psychologist who was then at Teacher's College at Columbia University, and Robert M. Krauss, then one of his students. Professor Deutsch, who had long been interested in conflicts and their resolution, had gotten the idea for the game during a trip to Italy, where he witnessed a marvelous scene: two enormous buses had met head-on at one of the narrow curves on the scenic Amalfi Drive between Salerno and Sorrento; it was impossible for them to pass. Each driver, with every gesture and invective at his command, was insisting that the other back up. Neither would budge.[10]

This was the genesis of the Acme-Bolt Trucking Game. A two-person game that involved bargaining and communication, it was an abstract affair with no rules. Each player was given a simplified map with two routes (see Fig. 1, p. 244): on one route, the Acme truck would be bound to collide with the Bolt truck; on the other route, the trucks could avoid collision, but they would be late in reaching their destinations. In addition, each person controlled a barrier that could be used to block or delay the other person's vehicle on the shorter route (the game is more fully described in Appendix note 2). That was all there was to it. By discussion, offers, and counteroffers, the players tried to resolve the problem of who would go ahead, who would back up, and how both could reach their destinations most efficiently.

Most of the players in Deutsch's study were strangers to each other, but it seemed to me that this bargaining game might help couples in treatment deal with unresolved conflicts that kept erupting during our sessions. I got together with Professor Deutsch, whose interest had been caught by my speculations about the secret games played by husbands and wives just as mine had been caught by his bargaining game. As a result, thirty couples I was treating played the Trucking Game over a six-week period.[11]

The impact on my patients was tremendous. As each

couple came into my office after the game-playing session, it was evident that something important had happened. Instead of the usual bitterness and bickering,
they were eagerly discussing something they had done
together, a game they had played. And as they talked
about what they had done in the game, there were stun-
ning flashes of enlightenment. They started to compare
certain actions to those that had occurred in other set-
tings and situations. The rules governing their relationships, each couple excitedly discovered, had been the
same. There was a pattern in their interaction. I could
recognize it now, and so could they.

Immediately treatment became somewhat easier. Now
we had something concrete to discuss. There were no
more red herrings, fewer accusations, fewer demands
that I take sides or adjudicate disputes, more willingness
to examine just what was going on within their own nuclear unit.

I was as excited as my patients. I had not expected the
bargaining game to trigger such recognition or yield so
much information. I immediately began thinking of how
much more information might be gained from a more
literal form of the game. Professor Deutsch encouraged
me to construct one. I decided to build a game that
would use toy electric trains.[12]

My first version consisted of two HO-gauge engines
and two sets of track. Each length of track, which approx-
imated the original Deutsch dual-truck routes, covered
half of a Ping-Pong-sized table. Each player had his own
engine and stretch of track, which forked to provide a
short and a long route, both leading to the same destination. Each player had an instrument panel with a lever for
start, stop, and reverse; buttons for the Alternate or Di-

rect routes; flashing lights that indicated collisions; a button that enabled the player to close a barrier and block his partner from reaching his destination, and another to reopen it.

The game has since undergone two major revisions. The first chiefly reduced its size so that it could be transported more easily for demonstration purposes. This was a simple matter of switching to N-gauge equipment, which reduced the game to bridge-table size.

The third version (see Figs. 2 and 3, p. 246) is considerably more sophisticated than the first two and is almost completely computerized. It includes an electric sign showing time elapsed during each trip and money earned or lost by each partner, information that previously had been announced by the tester. In the third version, the role of the tester has been rendered almost invisible so that the game players are less tempted to interact with the tester or put on some other act for the tester's benefit (as Julie reported she and Jim had tried to do), which dilutes the couple's observable interaction.

Another important new feature is that parameters of the game can be altered. The data that has been stored on integrated circuits is electronically transmitted to a central computer that analyzes it almost instantaneously. Then, based upon the pattern of interaction of the pair that is being tested, one or more appropriate changes in the situation can be introduced in order to "stress" their particular pattern of interaction. For example, if one person has always closed the barrier, this function could be inhibited, and if one person always took the Alternate Route, that option could be closed off. The entire sequence of events on each trip is recorded and can be studied for very fine details.[13]

So within fifteen or twenty minutes after a couple has completed the test, I have a breakdown in symbols and graph form of all the trips that make up the game. It shows just what they did: who took the Direct Route and how often, who took the Alternate Route and how often, who reversed, who used the barrier and how often, when they collided and who reversed, and how long each collision lasted.

This averages out to some four hundred separate items of information, which are listed trip by trip. This statistical printout is followed by the printout of a graph (see, for example, diagram on pp. 62–3) that shows in concrete form the pattern of interaction within the nuclear pair. It is a blueprint of their relationship, a faithful reproduction of how they have interacted with each other over the course of their marriage and at the present time.

What it all adds up to is that in an hour and a half, approximately the time it takes to play the Train Game and get the computer printouts, I can find out just what game a couple is playing—and what rules they are using to play it.

8

The Big Three, the Minor Four, and the Chaotic Eighth

What are these games that couples play? I refer to them as the Big Three, the Minor Four, and the Chaotic Eighth. These are not symphonies. They represent the eight patterns of human interaction, which had never been isolated, identified, codified, and subjected to statistical and psychiatric analysis until the Train Game provided the tool for this advance.

There are three major patterns, each of them quite individual; the Minor Four are combined patterns that incorporate two (and in one case, all three) of the Big Three, and the Chaotic Eighth is a maverick pattern that represents no more than 1.5 percent of all relationships.

The three patterns of the Big Three are: Dominant-Submissive, Cooperative, and Competitive.[14] And these represent about three-fifths (60 percent) of all marriages.

1. *The Dominant-Submissive Pattern.* As the name indicates, there is a leader and a follower within the nuclear couple. It is often quite difficult to spot the leader. He or she can be a sneaky tyrant enveloped in a guise of lamb-like meekness. There is another aspect to this pattern

that often leads novices astray. I call it the Flipflop Phenomenon.* The members of the Dominant-Submissive nuclear couple invariably exchange roles on a cyclical rotation (except in very rare cases in which no exchange is apparent). In other words, last month's dictator may be this week's slave, but the outside world is seldom cognizant of the switchover. The husband or wife who appears dominant to outsiders or even to other members of the family may be, in fact, the submissive partner for long periods of time. The role-change cycle is quite individual within each couple, but there is a definite cycle that can eventually be determined, somewhat akin to the variations of the tides. The couple usually has to be observed over a period of time before the full cycle is seen. In the Train Game, we find that in twenty to twenty-eight trips the cycle will usually be indicated, and in a few cases will be completely defined; with others, it may take a second or third go-round of the game—several months apart—to spot the cyclical pattern.

---

*When one sees a marriage in which one person is always collapsing—either physically or emotionally—it is usually a Dominant-Submissive relationship. A dramatic example of how the Flipflop Phenomenon works was provided by one couple in which the husband was in agony for months because of his back. All kinds of painful tests were performed on him to rule out this and that. Surgery was necessary. Six months after surgery, when he was well on the way to recovery, his wife "put her back out." She had a series of tests, spent time in traction, and finally underwent surgery. This was a striking instance of the Flipflop Phenomenon. This couple had demonstrated the Flipflop Phenomenon earlier, when the wife was pregnant with their first child. She had a difficult pregnancy. A few weeks after she was home from the hospital with the baby, the husband developed stomach ulcers. The Flipflop Phenomenon is not always as drastic as with this couple, of course.

Just slightly more than a quarter of all the cases I treat fall into the Dominant-Submissive pattern. This seems to reflect quite faithfully the proportion of Dominant-Submissive relationships in the married population in general.

One very important characteristic of the Dominant-Submissive pattern is that these couples seldom divorce. They may be happy, they may be miserable, but they stick together.

2. *The Cooperative Pattern.* One-fifth of all husbands and wives and other intimate couples fall into this category.

This is usually a placid interaction. These husbands and wives are thoughtful, considerate of each other, pleased to help the other, and on the whole enjoy what we have been taught to consider a very civilized relationship, with their give-and-take governed by good will. But in truth, "enjoy" may be the wrong word to apply to this relationship, for it can result in the dullest of marriages. There is little spice in the interaction within the nuclear couple. So little, in fact, that there is more extramarital experimentation by husband and wife than in any other group. It seems that there is just not enough going on within the couple to keep these seemingly well-adjusted partners sexually and emotionally involved, no matter how "fond" they may be of each other.

Divorce is not uncommon with these couples. There is one variation of the Cooperative pattern, which the Train Game zeroes in on, that invariably (or practically invariably) leads to divorce or separation. Julie and Jim were an example of that variation.

3. *The Competitive Pattern.* This is a shocker to many. Several family therapists resisted my findings on the Competitive pattern when they first heard about them,

only to come around to accepting them—sometimes re-
luctantly—on the basis of their own work with the Train
Game and their further study of my carefully docu-
mented observations.

We have given lip service for so long to the idea that
it is not "nice" or proper to compete, especially with
those you love, that this has come to assume the proportions of a natural law. Well, all I can say to that on the
basis of my work is: it's simply not so. The couples who
fall into the Competitive category, 14 percent, are never
bored with their marriages. The competition often
becomes so fierce that they are exhausted; that is a very
real problem. But the interaction is so real, so vital, so
close that these couples have no reason to complain, as
so many others do, that they fear life is passing them by,
that "there must be more to life than this." Quite to the
contrary, they are engaged with each other, excited, and
living life to the fullest, though not necessarily the happiest. As I said, the competition may be so rugged that
after a certain length of time, one or the other or both
can't stand it. Then there is illness and/or separation or
divorce unless the couple can be taught to turn down the
level of competition or—and I always try to help them do
this—learn one or more other ways of interacting so that
when the competition gets too intense, they can relax for
a while in the comfortable humdrum of a Cooperative
pattern, for instance.

The Minor Four are based on the Big Three. And the
combinations yield quite unexpected results at times.
The breakdown of this group, which represents roughly
a third of all marriages, is as follows:

1. *Dominant-Submissive/Competitive.* Approximately 16 percent of the couples I and my colleagues have tested belong to this group.

2. *Dominant-Submissive/Cooperative.* About 12 percent of the married population.

3. *Cooperative/Competitive.* Five percent.

4. *Dominant-Submissive/Cooperative/Competitive.* About 5 percent of the couples we have tested fall into this fascinating pattern. Theoretically, people who can command three major patterns of interacting with each other should be flexible enough to cope with most of the stresses of contemporary marriage. Unfortunately, this does not seem to hold true. This group is composed of couples whose partners are strongly attracted to each other but very often just can't seem to get along.

And then there is that maverick group, the Chaotic Eighth. As I reported earlier in this chapter, only about 1.5 percent of all the people I see in my practice exhibit this pattern of interaction.

Their interactions are seemingly without rhyme or reason, certainly appear to be without rules, which is the only rule that exists in this pattern. Chaotic Eighth relationships are not quite anarchic. Their only rule is that "There shall be no rule."

Some people tend to confuse personality with interaction. It is important to realize that there is no clear connection between personality traits and patterns of interaction. For example, let us take the case of a man whose first marriage clearly exhibited a Dominant-Submissive pattern. After his wife's death, he falls in love again and eventually remarries. His second wife possesses many personality characteristics of his first wife. She is an ebullient, outgoing, warm woman just like his first wife. But the interaction of this man and his second wife will not resemble that which existed between him and his first wife. First of all, the marriage may fall into some other pattern. And, second, if it does exhibit the characteristics of a Dominant-Submissive union, it will still be different. The pattern of interaction will be the same, but the cycles and the expression of the interaction will be different.

The fact that there are only eight patterns of interaction and the fact of the predictability of these patterns and the interactions within them become less terrifying to some people when I remind them that our planet, as every child who ever played the game of Twenty Questions accepts, is divided into *only* three categories—animal, vegetable, and mineral. But what a miraculous infinity of variations there is within each category!

9

Dominant-Submissive: The Primitive Interaction

Nothing in life is absolutely clear cut, black or white, right or wrong. And so it is with these categories. The Dominant-Submissive is the most primitive of all interactions, the one that underlies all others. In almost every intimate interaction, there is a hint, often the merest trace, of the Dominant-Submissive, an inheritance from our evolutionary past.

Dr. Jane Van Lawick-Goodall, whose study of chimpanzees illuminated several aspects of human behavior, has pointed out how strongly certain behavior patterns of the chimpanzee resemble those of man. Chimpanzee communities, for instance, show a "fairly well-defined dominance hierarchy," she has reported. This finding among others led her to accept as fact that "at some point in the distant past, man and chimpanzee shared a common ancestor. If this is true, we may assume that characteristics shared by modern man and modern chimpanzee were present in our stone-age ancestors."

One of those characteristics, without question, is the Dominant-Submissive pattern of interaction. "Domi-

nance is something of a conundrum in chimpanzee society," Dr. Lawick-Goodall writes. The rewards are not
quite clear, but "many chimpanzees do seem preoc-
cupied with raising their social status, while others are
less concerned and tend to keep out of the way."

To understand the dynamics of the other interaction
patterns, it is important to understand the very powerful
forces at work in the Dominant-Submissive pattern. The
graph on pages 62–3 shows a very typical Dominant-
Submissive pattern. It is the computer printout of how
one couple played the Train Game. In this case, the wife,
who is represented by the broken line, "won," having
made three times as much profit as her husband, who is
represented by the solid line. The figures along the bottom of the graph represent the trips that make up the
Train Game.

It is clear that the wife is the dominant partner in this
nuclear couple—at this time. She may be in a long dominant cycle. Once she established her preferred, profitable way of playing the Train Game, she persisted in it.
The chart shows that from the seventh trip on, she consistently finished first and won the larger share. Her husband also settled down into a steady pattern at the very
same point, the seventh trip. It is interesting to note,
however, that there is more unevenness in his game—
that dip, for instance, at the fifteenth trip, and the rise on
the eighteenth. It could be that this rise marked the end
of a cycle for him and that he was getting ready to go into
a dominant phase—the Flipflop Phenomenon described
above.

This graph, outlining just about the most primitive of
all Dominant-Submissive patterns, is interesting because
this couple had no collisions after the fifth trip and nei-

LEGEND FOR DIAGRAMS

The numbers 1–20 at the bottom of the graph refer to trips. An asterisk (*) in the line above indicates that one or more collisions occurred on that trip.

The numbers 0, 1, 2 in the three columns on the left indicate only which of the following choices of action a player took.

The numbers under BARRIER answer the question "Did the player use the barrier (close it to the other player)?" The answers are:

> 0: No
>
> 1: Yes, and was the first and/or only player to do so
>
> 2: Yes, and was the second player to do so

The second column, ROUTE AND ORDER OF FINISH, asks: "Which route did the player select? Did he or she finish first or second?" The answers are:

> 0: Alternate route
>
> 1: Direct route, and finished first
>
> 2: Direct route, and finished second

The third column, DIRECTION, asks: "In what direction did the player move his or her train?" The answers are:

> 0: Forward only
>
> 1: Forward, in reverse, and then forward again, with no route change
>
> 2: Forward, in reverse, changed route, and then forward again

Thus, on Trip 3 illustrated on pp. 62–3, the husband (X) did not use the barrier; he took the Direct route and finished first; during the trip he reversed but then continued on the Direct route. His choices are represented by the numbers 011. His wife (O) closed the barrier; she took the Direct route and finished second; she also reversed but then continued along the Direct route. Her choices are represented by the numbers 121. At some point or points, there were one or more collisions, as shown by the asterisk.

On any trip, one player is plotted above (toward the top of the graph) the other. This indicates that he/she finished first.

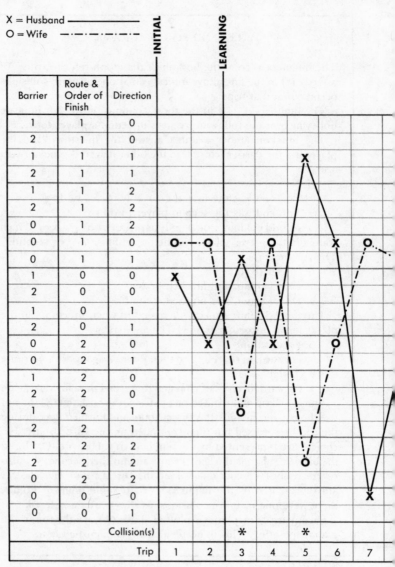

X = Husband ——————
O = Wife —·—·—·—·—

Barrier	Route & Order of Finish	Direction	INITIAL / LEARNING chart
1	1	0	
2	1	0	
1	1	1	
2	1	1	
1	1	2	
2	1	2	
0	1	2	
0	1	0	
0	1	1	
1	0	0	
2	0	0	
1	0	1	
2	0	1	
0	2	0	
0	2	1	
1	2	0	
2	2	0	
1	2	1	
2	2	1	
1	2	2	
2	2	2	
0	2	2	
0	0	0	
0	0	1	
		Collision(s)	* (trip 3), * (trip 5)
		Trip	1 2 3 4 5 6 7

This couple shows a Dominant-Submissive pattern of interaction. It emerges clearly from the seventh trip on. On the seventh, fifteenth, and eighteenth trips the husband took the Alternate Route. On all other trips he waited for

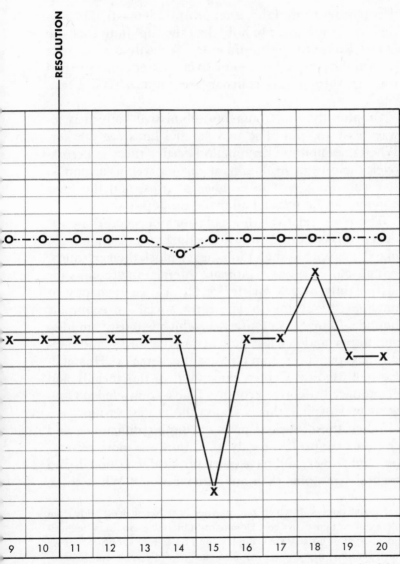

his wife to pass through the collision area before proceeding. On the eightu eenth trip he closed the barrier, but opened it to allow her to finish first. (For information on how to interpret this diagram, please refer to p. 61.)

ther partner caused the other any problem—that is, neither used the barrier to hold the other up. Both took the Direct Route to the destination. The wife always went first, and her husband submissively waited until she had traveled through the collision area until he could proceed.

Graphically, the Dominant-Submissive pattern is always easy to spot. The two parallel lines are the key. When the Flipflop Phenomenon occurs, there is a crossover; the previously dominant partner accepts a submissive role for a certain number of trips, and the lines continue to be parallel after the flipflop.

There are relatively few collisions between the partners in this pattern. Some do use the barriers, but others, like the couple in the graph, never block their partners.

This most prevalent intimate interaction accounts for just slightly over a quarter of all marriages, happy or unhappy. It seems to know no social or economic bounds. In my private practice, which is mostly middle- and upper-middle-class patients; in the lower- and middle-class patients whom I treat at the New York Hospital-Cornell Medical Center clinic; and in the socially and economically deprived couples I have counseled at Gouverneur Hospital, this is always the largest group.

When these nuclear pairs encounter difficulties and come to me professionally, then they are more miserable, unhappier, and have more physical, emotional, and mental symptoms than any other group.* When these

---

*Most couples in which one partner is either a drug addict, an alcoholic or depressive test Dominant-Submissive. So, in my experience, do most homosexual couples, but I have treated only five or six such liaisons, not enough to allow me to draw valid conclusions. Whether all homosexual pairs would test out as Dominant-Submissive or whether, given a statistically significant sample, they would fall

couples tell me about their problems, it is like being shown a raw wound. There is no doubt but that these people hurt. They are truly, exquisitely miserable. They hurt so much that they can't stand it. They threaten divorce or separation, but rarely carry through with the threat. Vituperation, abuse, even actual violence are characteristic of the unhappier unions in this category.

I used to think that it was the Submissives who were the losers in these pairs and suffered most from rage and depression, but experience has taught me that both suffer, and often the Dominant suffers more. It is important to recognize that the submissive person is not just giving in to the other. He is *insisting* on being submissive. Even when the Dominant may suggest, "Let's change this," the Submissive will literally not permit the change. He may move—but stay one step below his partner. Thus, he forces the other to remain dominant. From a philosophical point of view one might say that the person who is as far down as he can be has a certain advantage. There is no place to go but up.

I am sometimes asked if in these days of Women's Liberation and consciousness raising, the Dominant-Submissive pattern will not fade away. My response is that my questioners are guilty of sexist thinking. The incidence of this pattern may eventually decrease, but not for this reason. The dominant role is not taken by men any more than the submissive role is usually taken by women in our culture. The roles do not carry sexual connotations.

And, in actual fact, the reverse is closer to the truth. The woman is more often the Dominant than the Sub-

---

into the same percentages and patterns as heterosexual couples still has to be determined.

missive, probably because in our culture women are permitted to be weak as well as strong and to dominate through weakness. It is not yet culturally approved for a man to say, "Oh, I can't do that, you'll have to do it for me," which is one method of domineering. The woman also has the choice of straightforward dominance, of saying, "We will do this or that," which can often be translated as *"You* will do this or that."

In contrast, the man can only dominate by strength. It may be that some future reassessment will yield another definition for the "weaker sex." This tag may shift from the female to the male.

The Flipflop Phenomenon allows each partner to have a turn at dominance in some cycle that the nuclear pair finds right for itself. This Flipflop is a most effective, built-in antistress mechanism. It may be the reason for the longevity of these unions. The couple instinctively swap dominance roles when the tensions grow too great to be tolerated. And a good thing that is, for no matter how miserable the partners are, most Dominant-Submissive couples won't be split.

The Dominant-Submissives who come to me for help are, by and large, older than couples with other patterns of interaction. About a decade older on the average. This is an indication, I believe, of the strength of the interactive bond. In some cases, these couples are not even able to admit that they are having trouble until their misery is so gross, so all pervading, that it is no longer possible to deny that something is very wrong. In other cases, the full impact of their unhappiness does not strike until the children are grown and start leaving home for college, marriage, or work. More than the expected share of "twenty-year fractures"—divorces after the children are grown—that I see fall into the Dominant-Submissive pattern. While the children were home, they provided relief from the oppressive closeness of the relationship. But when the children leave, husband and wife are locked into their interaction with no way of ameliorating the stress.[15]

Treatment is difficult, because these couples resist change so strongly. Often, just when I think I have made a breakthrough, have succeeded in introducing some small change that may make their interaction less wounding and more comfortable (I think of it as introducing a drop of oil into a tight joint), they stop treatment. Simply cut it off. The threat of change, of even the slightest psychic separation, cannot be tolerated. They would prefer to be miserable. And so they drop out.

The changes I introduce into a Dominant-Submissive relationship often seem ludicrously small, but each looms like a mountain to the couple.

I may begin by asking the husband, "What goes on when you come home from work? Before you walk in the door? Before you eat dinner?" Or I will start at the beginning of the day and try to disentangle the couple's actions. "When do you eat breakfast? With whom? What do you eat?" And I will go right through the minutiae of their lives to "What side of the bed do you sleep on? How much distance is there between you in bed?"

I then try to introduce nonthreatening changes that may introduce a new perspective or ease some of the tenseness. For instance, I suggested that one pair start by literally giving themselves a new perspective—swapping sides of the bed. They agreed, but after two months of sleeping on the "wrong" side, they sheepishly reported that they had returned to their accustomed position.

They had not been able to accept the change. In fact, during those two months, they had never gotten around to shifting the contents of their bedside tables.

I consider treatment a success if the pair has been able to restructure the relationship and interact with each other more flexibly, or when some couples attain the strength to escape from a destructive relationship. In either case, it takes a very long time. Only by advancing at a psychological snail's pace are the partners able to accept even the most minor changes or to discover that they can exist without each other. In the process, their perceptions of themselves, of their partner, and of the world are changed.

Often the first indication of improvement in any marriage comes from the couple's children. This is particularly true of the Dominant-Submissive relationship, which tends to produce disturbed children. The tension caused by the superintimacy envelops the child as well as the parent. He has a sense that this stressful structure is being held together by him. This is not true, of course, but the very idea is a terrible burden and can cause all sorts of neurotic disturbances in children.

When a Dominant-Submissive pair's relationship is improving, it is quite usual for them to come in one day and remark, "I don't know what has happened to our son, but he is acting much better these days." It is as if the children pick up the change before the parents are even aware that it has occurred.

Having said all this, it is important to point out that the majority of Dominant-Submissive marriages are *not* miserable. Quite the contrary. It is simply that the largest group of couples who seek marital therapy are in the Dominant-Submissive category. Since the same proportion of Dominant-Submissive marriages seems to exist in the married population as a whole, and since only a fraction of that population seeks help for ailing marriages, it follows that the majority of Dominant-Submissive couples are happy enough.*

Another question I am often asked is, "If these unions are so stressful, how do you account for the preponderance of happy-enough Dominant-Submissive unions?" The explanation is simplicity itself. There are millions of people who are quite content to be followers; they have paired with other millions of people who are quite content to be leaders. And the Flipflop Phenomenon gives them a chance to trade off. These relationships work out beautifully. And most Dominant-Submissive unions are satisfactory and fulfilling.[16]

*According to a massive survey, in *Life* magazine, 20 percent of American couples rate their marriages as "all right" to "unhappy." And of that 20 percent, 53 percent (just over half) had sought counseling. In other words, about 10 percent of all married couples seek professional help. On this basis, one can speculate that unhappy Dominant-Submissive pairings account for approximately 12 to 15 percent of all marriages. How do I arrive at this figure? Is not the percentage for unhappy Dominant-Submissives closer to 5 percent, since this pattern represents approximately one quarter of all marriages? No. My explanation for this seeming discrepancy lies in that 47 percent of more or less unhappy couples who have not sought marital therapy. Since it is characteristic of Dominant-Submissives to resist change, and since even the act of seeking help represents change, one must accept that the representation of Dominant-Submissives in this unhappy yet resistant group is probably disproportionately high. But until the day arrives when all couples routinely take the Ravich Interpersonal Game/Test, just as they submit to a blood test in order to obtain a marriage license, these figures must remain speculative.

Several very comforting predictions may therefore be made about these unions. Only about 12 to 15 percent of those pairs who test out as Dominant-Submissive will be actively unhappy. Few of these marriages will end up in the divorce court. Most will be happy enough.

If the nuclear pair can find ways of relieving the potentially stressful closeness, they can look forward to a mutually rewarding life. And many of the couples whose stresses have turned their lives into living hells can find ways of alleviating these stresses caused by overintimacy and carve out a tolerable life for themselves.

10

Dominant-Submissive: Victoria and Disraeli

DISRAELI: Let's go.

VICTORIA: I don't know. I'm there. I guess. Have you started? Are you there? What's happened?

DISRAELI: We had a collision.

VICTORIA: Now it's going again. I don't know what happened. We had a collision? How can we have a collision if we're both going in the same direction?

DISRAELI: Listen, the next time, why don't you take the Direct and I'll take the Alternate. And—well, let's see what happens.

VICTORIA: (Silence)

DISRAELI: Are you on Direct? We had a collision again. All right. Just stay where you are and I'll back up. Did you get there? Huh?

VICTORIA: Yes.

DISRAELI: Why don't you let me know when you get there?

VICTORIA: Let's work independently this time.

DISRAELI: Why work independently? You can't work anything out that way. What this whole thing requires is coordination. If we stopped talking, there would be a collision every time. You won't know where I am and I won't know where you are.

VICTORIA: What do you want me to press?

DISRAELI: I don't know. I wonder about this barrier. I don't see any point in putting up the barrier. It simply . . . I'd like to see how it works.

VICTORIA: Why don't you push it? It's the only way to find out how it works.

DISRAELI: Please try to think. The object is both of us winning.

VICTORIA: But there are collisions when we both try to win.

DISRAELI: I suppose that's it. Who's going to win? But . . . No! It can't be. There must be a way for both of us to win.

VICTORIA: There's only one winner. Two people can't win in a race.

DISRAELI: They can if they're a team. That's the idea! A team can win! There can only be one winner if you and I compete. But if we are a team, we can win. The question is how can two win without a collision?

VICTORIA: Why don't we both try the Alternate? We haven't done that.

DISRAELI: Yes, we have. It took forever. Remember?

VICTORIA: Do you want me to take it?

DISRAELI: What for? There's nothing to be gained that way. You will lose more than I can make.

DISRAELI: Well, let's *have* a collision. Just to have something to experiment with. Okay? Now! (*Collision*) Okay. We collide. I'm backing up. You go ahead.
VICTORIA: That's the highest profit we've had. Twenty-one cents. And we had a collision.

These Kafkaesque fragments of dialogue between a husband and wife (I call them Disraeli and Victoria for reasons that will become clear very shortly) are excerpts from their tape-recorded comments as they played the Train Game. They are not the casual trivialities they might seem at first reading, but reflections of the couple's basic interactions.

Victoria and Disraeli were one of the couples who eventually came to terms with their straightforward Dominant-Submissive pattern of interaction. And, as in many instances of this pattern, the partner who appeared to be dominant was, in actuality, submissive for the greater part of the time.

When Sam and Janet Middleton came to me, they were middle-aged with grown children. Their youngest was nineteen, the oldest twenty-five. They had been unhappy for years and had sought help a few years earlier with another therapist. Now their problems had escalated and the therapist threw up his hands, said he had done all he could for them, and referred them to me.

My usual practice is to interview a couple for half an hour on their first visit. It is just a very brief getting-acquainted period. On the first visit, they told me about themselves, about their children, about their inability to function effectively together and underlined their desire to improve their marriage.

One of Janet's complaints was that Sam was always

telling her what to do. "I wish he'd get off my back," she said. And Sam was often furious at Janet for not doing as he told her. But what he resented most of all was that he would instruct her to do such and such—invite a certain couple to dinner, take the car to the garage, make plane reservations for their vacation—and Janet would not do it. Not only wouldn't she do it, but she never told him that she would not—or had not. So time after time, Sam would confidently expect that a business contact and his wife would be coming to dinner or that he could pick up plane tickets downtown that Janet had ordered only to discover that Janet had done nothing about it.

After this short session, we made an appointment for the following week and then they were taken to the testing room to play the Train Game.

Later that day, I looked at their graph. It was a clear Dominant-Submissive pattern. I had expected this on the basis of their pregame interview. And as I listened to the taped verbal interaction of Janet and Sam Middleton, I formed a very strong impression of the roles they had assigned themselves as a couple, assigned themselves without ever having discussed the assignment.

What I heard was Sam talking, talking, talking. He was always making suggestions about what they should do next, thinking up different things to try. His wife, on the other hand, was quite taciturn. Occasionally she would say, "Okay," and do what he suggested. But more often Janet would say nothing and continue on her own sweet way. Or she would do just what Sam had suggested, but without saying a word to indicate that this was what she was doing.

Sam never knew what her silence meant. Was it agreement? Or disagreement? As I listened, I realized that

Janet had assumed the prerogatives of royalty. And Sam was her advisor.

At our postgame session, both Sam and Janet started talking animatedly about the game. Sam felt that if Janet had paid more attention to his suggestions, they would have attained a better score.

"I feel like a quarterback calling the plays," Sam said, "but nobody is listening to me."

I turned to Janet and asked, "Well, what position would you say *you* play on this team?"

She thought a moment and said, "I guess I'm the center."

I was momentarily stunned. Then I realized that the center is the pivotal position, in a curious way more important than the quarterback, because if the quarterback called the plays but the center didn't pass him the ball, there would be no play.

Sam's response to Janet's description was, "Sometimes I think of her as the kid who owns the football."

This brief exchange opened up a vast range of interaction for discussion. Until they played the Train Game, they had never analyzed the role each played in the marriage. But as soon as they had the game to relate to, it seemed the most natural thing in the world for them to pinpoint just what each did in their relationship.

After a few sessions, I decided to introduce the other analogy that seemed more appropriate to their relationship than the football one. "It seems to me," I said, "that Janet considers herself above it all, a kind of queen. She deigns to listen to your advice. And when she deems it convenient, she takes the advice. But she never feels compelled to thank her prime minister—or even to tell him what she has decided to do. After all, this is the duty of his office—to advise the queen."

A lot of back-and-forth ensued about this. Janet protested vehemently at first that she never acted like royalty. But Sam was thoughtful. At the end of the session he remarked, "Well, I guess there's plenty of responsibility for the prime minister."

Some time later, he said that he had recognized during this session that he had always been knocking himself out trying to become king, to be the dominant one in the relationship. But the prime minister never becomes king.

Life became somewhat easier for this latter-day Victoria and Disraeli after they came to terms with these roles that they had never recognized before. They were never able to adopt another pattern of interaction, but the fact of learning just what was going on between them and identifying their roles, those roles they had been playing for the twenty-nine years of their marriage, seemed to provide some easing in the relationship.

This was a typical Dominant-Submissive pattern in many ways, but Janet (Victoria) was the secret ruler. Everyone tended to think that Sam was boss because he was forever telling his wife what to do. The truth was that Janet ruled; the power of decision lay with her.

The Flipflop Phenomenon, so characteristic of this pattern, was not as pronounced with Janet and Sam as with other couples, but it existed. There was never a chance that Sam was going to be king or that Janet would accept the lesser role of prime minister. Yet, even in this rigid pattern, there were times when Sam was the leader, when the queen accepted and acted upon the prime minister's advice. Then Sam could indeed feel that he was the power behind the throne. The *real* power. This satisfaction gave him enough psychic space or freedom to allow him to continue cheerfully in his subordinate position until the next time Janet deigned to bow to his counsel.

As a therapist, I think my most significant contribution was helping Sam to stop banging his head against the wall. He slowly began to realize that there was no point in trying to get on equal terms with his wife, because she simply would not allow it. He had to learn that—and accept it. And Janet had to learn just what she was doing. She had been quite unconscious of the regal stance she had adopted in her marriage.

Once the two of them were quite clear about what they were doing, what was going on between them, then they could begin to adapt to it. Sam could console himself, "Well, the queen is just a figurehead. It's the prime minister who has the brains." Whether it was true or not did not really matter. The important thing was that it helped him to adjust to a situation that could not be changed within the structure of this particular relationship.

Would it have been possible to predict this Victoria/ Disraeli pattern thirty years ago? I believe so. And I believe that both Sam and Janet could have enjoyed thirty much more rewarding years if they had understood the dynamics of their relationship from the very beginning.

Two options were open to them. One was to decide not to marry. The other was to decide to adapt to the stresses of the marriage.

I believe, with hindsight, that I would have advised them not to marry. Sam, particularly, was miserable in the marriage. He was frustrated by it, caged in it. And saw no way of getting out of it. Marriage with another woman could have given him a more satisfying life.

The second choice might have been much more difficult to carry out. I am firmly convinced that there is only one difference between happy and unhappy Dominant-Submissive marriages and that is a differing capacity to adapt, either a more or a less pronounced flexibility. Partners who can accept the rigid conditions of the Dominant-Submissive relationship tend to live happily enough ever after. But those who find themselves almost literally being crushed by the unremitting rigidity of the interaction exhibit a degree of misery that should not have to exist.

To ask engaged couples to change their plans because their interaction does not seem conducive to a satisfying marriage may not meet with much success today. But I am convinced that the time is almost here when people will have such a yearning for stability, that they will understand how destructive the present escalation of the divorce rate is to society and the family, which after all is the nucleus of society, that they will want to take every precaution that will ensure them a good marriage.

If Janet and Sam had come to me asking if they would have had a good marriage, I think that I would have told them the odds were against it. Janet was so overpowering. Dominant-Submissive interactions are so unimpregnable to change. I would have had to say that the degree of flexibility exhibited by this couple would have to be of the highest order. Why not try for something better?

11

Dominant-Submissive: The Hit-and-Runners

One variation of the Dominant-Submissive pattern that puts me in a state of alert almost always points to some form of addiction: drugs, alcohol, food—even work addiction. And talk addiction. I call it the Hit-and-Run variation.

The Train Game invariably pinpoints the addict while he is in the grip of his addiction; it is less reliable with the addict who has temporarily shaken the habit—the alcoholic between binges, for instance.

The Collinses were almost good-looking. He would have been if it had not been for the trace of weakness and petulance in his face. And she would have been beautiful if she could have lost twenty-five to thirty pounds—and wiped the faintly vindictive expression off her face. To hear them talk during their initial, pregame visit the only trouble with their marriage was Glenna Collins' overeating. Paul was graphically articulate on how Glenna was turning herself into a two-ton tank and losing all her appeal.

Glenna protested, "But I'm on a diet."

"You've been on a diet for five years," Paul shouted at her. "And you've gone off every diet the day you started it."

He calmed down and turned to me. "Glenna hides food," he said, "the way an alcoholic stashes away bottles. She says she's on a diet and all she has for dinner is half a cup of cottage cheese and a quart of diet soda. Then I find her in the kitchen bolting down a half-pound Swiss chocolate bar or I find an empty Oreo box in the wastebasket. Whenever I wake up at night and Glenna's not there on her side of the bed, I know she's in the kitchen sneaking something to eat. And to tell the truth, I don't much care anymore. Who'd want to make love to that lump of blubber?" He was cruel. And Glenna's vindictive look became more pronounced. Their life appeared to be a series of confrontations over Glenna's inability to lose weight.

Their graph (see pp. 82–3) showed the Hit-and-Run variation of the Dominant-Submissive pattern. It worked this way. Each took the Direct Route. There was a collision—and Paul backed up instantly. This was the pattern through all of their trips. Sometimes he backed up and waited for Glenna to proceed; then he would start up again and finish second. At other times, he would back up and take the Alternate Route. It is like the hit-and-run driver who does not dare face the consequences of the accident. Unlike the usual Dominant-Submissive pattern, their graph was full of collisions. And the diagram of their interactions, instead of showing two steady lines with possibly a crossover or Flipflop, was more like the surface of the ocean (Glenna) and the jagged peaks of the ocean floor (Paul).

Paul ran so fast after a collision that Glenna didn't

even know that he had hit. It is possible to flick the Reverse switch of the Train Game so quickly that one's partner may miss the red collision light just in the blink of an eye. This happened repeatedly with the Collinses. Glenna would complete her trip oblivious to the fact that there had been a collision and that Paul had backed up. It was all spelled out very clearly on the computer print-out, however, and when I showed them the printout at a postgame session, Glenna was honestly astonished.

When there was a collision, Paul never mentioned it. They went on talking, carrying on a conversation that had nothing to do with what was happening between them. Nor did they remark that Glenna was always ahead on each game and Paul was always losing. This last fact puzzled me. It was clear that Glenna had a food addiction. So, based on my previous experience, Glenna should have been the loser, not Paul. She had admitted that she could not stop her compulsive eating. What was going on here?

Could it be that another variant pattern was emerging, for the first time? Something seemed to contradict my previous findings. Why was Paul the loser if Glenna was the addict?

Both husband and wife were politely interested in my report of the diagnostic findings of the game and my explanation of the graph. I pointed to the consistent peaks, which represented Paul's backing up after each collision. "What happened?" I asked. "How come Glenna always won?"

Glenna looked blank. She had no idea, literally no idea at all, why she had come out ahead on every single trip. That conformed to the pattern. In these hit-and-run games, the winner usually *is* unaware. Or he may wonder

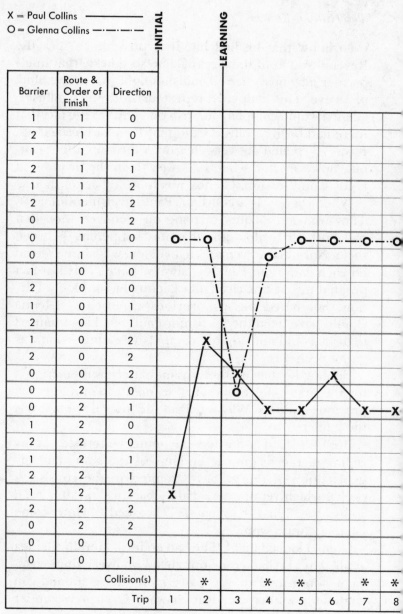

X = Paul Collins ——————
O = Glenna Collins —·—·—·—

This is a pure Dominant-Submissive pattern. Paul reverses away from the collisions, which occur on almost every trip. (For information on how to interpret this diagram, please refer to p. 61.)

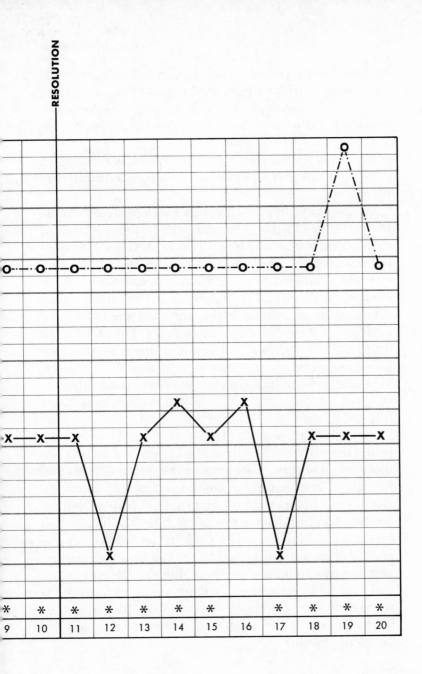

vaguely "How come?" and then conclude that "Oh, something must be rigged in the game."

Finally, Glenna replied, "Well, I thought Paul was getting kind of sour there for a while, but then he didn't say anything, so I forgot about it."[17]

But the question was still there. Why was Paul such a persistent loser? It was his wife who had the addiction. Or was it?

I took a stab and asked him how much he usually drank in the course of a day. That unleashed a helter-skelter of words. Paul was an alcoholic. The Train Game had spotted it accurately. There was no new variation here. Paul was more addicted to alcohol than his wife was to food. He knew as much about stashing away bottles for sneaky drinks as she did about hiding the food she craved.

Here was a case of a consistent loser. Time after time he lost. Each trip was a relentless duplication of the previous failure. There was a great deal of fear here. What the game reflected was Glenna's refusal or inability to confront their real life problem. Glenna was more frightened than her husband.

Paul, after all, was involved enough to bring up the problem of her overeating and increasing obesity, even though in a bitterly cruel manner. He loved Glenna and he wanted her to stop turning herself into a mammoth. But Glenna had not mentioned Paul's drinking. Neither had he. And this despite the fact that his alcoholism had brought him close to losing his job. He had lost several contracts because of his drinking. His firm had warned him that this could not continue. But the closest Glenna and Paul had ever come to talking about his alcoholism was when, after a binge, she would refer to it as one of his "attacks," or his "migraine." They never faced the problem together.

Addiction is hard to treat. I felt that if I could help them to lessen the pressures of this unrelenting Dominant-Submissive pattern the surcease might diminish the force that drove them to their separate escapes. It is important to point out now that Glenna and Paul were somewhat unusual in that their graph did not indicate a single Flipflop. This was another corroboration of the terrible pressure of the rigid pattern they were locked into. Glenna was always winning—and miserable; Paul was always losing—and miserable. But I was worried about Paul. No one can stand losing forever.

As we worked together, I encouraged Paul and Glenna to talk about his drinking. I wanted to change the focus of their interaction from *her* addiction to *their* addictions. And several weeks later I detected some changes, an easier atmosphere within the nuclear couple. After several months had elapsed and Paul had been on the wagon, without a single relapse, I suggested that they be retested. They agreed.

This time their graph showed several Flipflops, occasions when the pattern of their play was reversed. Paul would win occasionally, because Glenna now, much more aware, started backing up once in a while after a collision so that he could continue unimpeded. The first couple of times this happened Paul was bewildered. He literally could not understand why he had suddenly stopped losing and begun winning. The experience was frightening.

After several more months of treatment, they themselves suggested they would like to play the Train Game again. They saw it as a way to measure progress. This time there was a definite Flipflop cycle. Paul would win a trip or two, Glenna would win a whole streak of trips, five or six. Then Paul would be the winner for two or three trips. It was a faithful reflection of how they had become more aware of each other. Now each partner was quite sensitive to what the other was doing and feeling: a dramatic contrast to their first test, in which Glenna through fear of facing Paul's alcoholism had simply sailed through each trip without knowing or caring what was going on.

I'd like to report that the Collinses are cured, sober and thin, but that would not be the truth. They are still married and are finding more security and more solace in the relationship than before. Paul attends a therapy group of alcoholics and former alcoholics. As with most couples in the Dominant-Submissive pattern, I am convinced Paul and Glenna would be lost without each other, even if their mutual life is far from a storybook marriage.

If Glenna and Paul had taken the Train Game test before they were married, what would have been predicted? Could their addictions have been foreseen? And if so, how would a therapist have counseled them?

The addiction syndrome, I'm convinced, would have been present during their courtship days, and would have been presented clearly by the Train Game graph. We know, from their own testimony, that Glenna was not overweight when they were married, so there would not have been that momentary puzzle of "Addiction, addiction, who's got the addiction?" The answer would clearly have been Paul.

If I were that hypothetical therapist who counseled them premaritally, I would have asked Glenna if she were aware that Paul was an alcoholic. If she was, I would have asked, "Why are you marrying this guy?" Her answer (based on my experience with other addicts and their wives) might have been, "Because he needs me. And I'm sure that when he's married, he'll stop drinking. He just needs someone to love him."

"You'll be his addiction then," I would have pointed out. "And not only that, it is a fact that addiction breeds addiction."

I would have tried to prevent this marriage. The medical and psychiatric professions have not chalked up a high rate of success in the treatment of addictions. At best, they substitute a less harmful addiction for a harmful one. And as I told Glenna in that hypothetical conversation, addiction *does* breed addiction. Today she is the living proof of this statement.

Would I have succeeded in preventing the marriage? Possibly not. In fact, probably not. The climate of marriage, of society itself, was different when Glenna and Paul were married. Today, I think I and other professionals using the Train Game to diagnose couples' interaction patterns may be more forceful in counseling such unhealthy pairings.

And if so, this means that eventually the proportion of Dominant-Submissive marriages may shrink. The Dominant-Submissive pattern is the traditional one, marriage "as it should be." Instead of traditional, I like to refer to it as "primitive," because it is the survival interaction of earlier days, when it was essential that the tribe instantly obey its leader when danger threatened. Today, survival is a more complicated affair demanding a more complicated set of interactions. There will always be Dominant-Submissive marriages, but I look forward to the time when they can be "defused," the destructive elements isolated.

This does not mean that these partners are going to

be left without mates. As I explained earlier, a man or woman's intimate interaction varies from person to person, depending on the nuclear "fit." The man who might be crushingly dominating in one pairing may be a perfect lamb demonstrating reasonableness and cooperation in another pairing. With guidance, unhappy marriages may be avoided and potentially happy unions pinpointed. While the Train Game is not an infallible instrument, falling in love is even less of an indication of what one may expect of a marriage. Ask anyone who's been there.

12

Dominant-Submissive: The Noisy Martyr

The martyr is a familiar marital character. Put upon, subservient, self-sacrificing—and a bore with her* incessant complaints about how she gives up everything for the sake of others who, of course, never appreciate her sacrifices. In actuality, the martyr is often the very model of a rigid domestic dictator.

The Springfields are opposites. He's from the Far West; she's a born and bred New Yorker. He's laconic, a Gary Cooper of a man; she's a nonstop talker who keeps the airspace between them full of chatter.

Elise says, "If I didn't talk, Ted would never say a word."

That would be all right with Ted. He likes it quiet. His idea of what a woman should be (and one must make allowances for a man in his fifties) is pretty, obedient— and quiet. Elise feels that she meets the first two requirements, and she points out that, although she does talk a

*In my experience, the martyr is usually, although not always, the wife.

lot, Ted is the boss and she spends all her time trying to please him.

"I do everything he tells me to do," she said. "I wear what he wants me to wear. I cook what he asks me to cook. I buy what he . . ." At this point in her recital of her unquestioning obedience, Ted interrupted. He winked at me and said, "I suppose you're going to tell the doctor you only go to the bathroom when I tell you to."

Elise was flustered and quiet for a few seconds; then she started up again. "You see what I mean, Doctor?" she asked. "He's always cutting me off. He doesn't want to talk. And he doesn't want me to talk."

"I don't like all that chatter," Ted said firmly.

In this pregame session, I learned that Ted did not like his wife's perpetual yak-yak—and he said so—and that Elise, who complained that she never knew what Ted was thinking, paid no attention to his signal that he couldn't stand "all that chatter." It was also clear that she would never be able to find out what he was thinking because she was doing so much talking that he never had a chance. And Elise was right in one respect: Ted was so silent that it was almost an invitation to her to talk in order to get something going between them.

The following day when I listened to the tape of their comments as they played the Train Game, I had to smile. Elise talked her way through all the trips. Ted made an occasional comment, but he probably uttered no more than twenty-five or thirty words, all of them on the order of "What?" "Yeah." "Sure." "Nope." "Uh-huh." There was no substantive communication on his part.

The game they played graphed out to a Dominant-Submissive pattern. It was not difficult to put one's finger on the dominant partner: Elise came out ahead. There had been three Flipflops, during which Ted was the winner for three trips, then for another series of three trips, and toward the end for two trips.

Ted wasn't top dog, no matter what Elise said. And what's more, he did not want to be. Although his upbringing had been such that superficially he did believe that a woman should be pretty, obedient, and quiet, he just gave lip service to the word "obedient." His natural inclination was for a more giving, more equal relationship than the one he found himself in. Elise, however, insisted on being almost slavishly obedient, and she liked to point out to me, to him, to her friends, and to her relatives just how oppressed she was. The truth was that this talkative martyr almost literally ordered her husband to "oppress" her.

Their interaction during therapy further confirmed the graph. I watched Ted evolve from a laconic head of the family to a rather tender man who yearned for a marriage that was more satisfying and fulfilling and for a wife who didn't insist he act like a Victorian paterfamilias. And then, time after time, I observed Elise swing into action with her sweet martyrdom, refusing to respond to Ted's signals—partly because she could not stop talking long enough to receive them—and thus freezing him back into his strong, silent role. Every time he showed signs of breaking out of this typecasting, she shoved him back into it.

The treatment of this aspect of their case was brutally simple. I pointed out to Elise that she could initiate a change in the structure of their relationship simply by shutting up. I told her to stop talking unless she had something important to say.

Ted looked shocked at this order, but Elise promptly responded, "You mean it's all right to tell him that the house is on fire but that I shouldn't bother about telling him that his fly isn't zipped?"

It worked. A few weeks later, after an unusually productive session, I congratulated Elise on her new self-restraint. She had really quieted down. The result had been that Ted was able to bring out some of the feelings that he had never voiced before. Elise's silence proved to be as powerful as her chatter. It forced Ted to talk—talk about his feelings and his needs, the very thing that Elise had thought she had been trying to get him to do for years. When I congratulated her, she said, "I'm beginning to realize how I was always sending Ted conflicting messages. I kept telling him I wanted him to talk to me, but I never gave him his share of air time."

As often happens with a Dominant-Submissive couple, this change in their interaction threw them into a tailspin. Suddenly they began coming into their sessions complaining about all sorts of problems: Their sex life was no good; they fought all the time; Elise was spending too much money; Ted was working too hard. I pointed out that there had been a major shift in their interaction, something that could be likened to major surgery or an earthquake. It would take time for everything to settle down and for the altered system to get into gear.

A few weeks later, Ted called and said that he and Elise had decided to stop therapy temporarily. I have not heard from them since. This is absolutely typical of the Dominant-Submissive pattern. This nuclear couple resists change. They are dug in. And when change does take place, it terrifies them; they don't know how to cope with it. I would guess that Ted and Elise reverted to the syndrome of the Noisy Martyr.

Could one have predicted the course of this marriage if Ted and Elise had taken the Train Game test during their courtship? Not in all its detail, certainly, but I believe that a professional with an understanding of the patterns of interactions could have outlined some steps they would have to make to ease the tensions that would indeed have been predictable.

This should have been a most satisfactory marriage, for if ever a couple were "made for each other," Ted and Elise were that couple. Elise, who came from a rather carefree, artistic family, found in Ted's quiet competence the kind of stability she had always craved. And Ted, despite his liking for quiet, relished Elise's vivacity and outgoing temperament. The very chatter that he objected to was part of her charm for him.

If they could have been helped to understand that the very meshing of their needs created an almost unbearable closeness (this was one of those cases where I like to think of treatment as introducing a drop of oil into the machinery), they could probably have handled the inevitable friction fairly easily.

A therapist trained in counseling engaged couples on the basis of their interactive pattern might have counseled Ted along these lines. "Look," he might have said, "Elise is exactly what you need to leaven your approach to life. She provides the fun and sparkle you admire. But there are times when that chatterbox quality that you find so engaging is going to rub you the wrong way.

"At those times, you are going to have to remind yourself that this is the price of closeness. When this happens and you get so that you can't stand it, you will have to put a little distance between yourself and Elise. Go off by yourself. Go to a movie or a museum or take a long walk. Go bowling with a friend. If the tension is really high, you might go on a camping trip. Something like that.

"In other words, give yourself occasional respites. Don't think of them as 'separations,' but as vacations from intimacy."

The same advice would have been appropriate for Elise. "There will be times," a therapist might have told her, "when the very stability that you admire so much in Ted will get on your nerves. If you face the fact that this is bound to happen, it won't seem like the end of the world—or of your marriage—when it does. You will be able to recognize it for what it is—too much closeness. The remedy for this is to put some distance between you."

If I had been that hypothetical therapist, I would have advised Elise to keep on working after she got married so that she would have an outlet for some of her exuberance and not pour it all on Ted. I would also have advised her to follow her natural inclinations and maintain a wide circle of friends so that when she and Ted were having closeness problems, she would have friends to talk out her feelings with. This, in fact, would have helped a lot. Elise gave up many of her friends in the early years of marriage in deference to Ted's wish to have peace and quiet at home. If they had realized that a closeness problem would exist and create friction, they could have worked out some way for Elise to maintain her friendships, possibly by having one evening a week when she would visit friends or play bridge without Ted, or one night every week or so when she would have her friends at home and Ted could join them or not as he pleased—without any hurt feelings.

This was a case where just a little nudge early on would have set the marriage on the right track. And, although

Ted and Elise broke off therapy rather abruptly and somewhat prematurely, I think that their perceptions had already been somewhat retrained and that they were beginning to give each other a little more emotional elbow room.

13

Dominant-Submissive:
Variation in Black

All the black couples I have treated have fallen into the Dominant-Submissive pattern in one or another of its several variants. While it is impossible to draw any valid generalization from this, the fact is that I have yet to see more than one exception to this. The woman, except in that one case, has always been Dominant. There is always a depression in the man. Even though he has overcome many of the social and economic barriers of this still racist society, it seems that he cannot very easily break out of the pattern of submission in marriage. At this writing, however, neither I nor those of my colleagues who have adopted the Train Game as a diagnostic tool have tested a large enough sample of black couples to justify any generalizations. This is up to future study.

A typical couple—typical in their interaction—were Joshua and Melitta Baker. Josh was a pharmacist. Melitta had worked as a secretary until their son was born. They had been referred to me by the doctor who had been treating Josh for narcotics addiction, an occupational hazard of pharmacy.

Josh had been in and out of the hospital three times for drug addiction. Melitta was constantly threatening to leave him, take Josh Junior with her, and never let him see his son again. Their whole life together was crumbling—sexually, financially, emotionally. Melitta said it was impossible to respect Josh any more, although she claimed she still loved him. And even though he had been off drugs for almost six months, she didn't trust him to stay "clean." And Josh, well, he reminded me of nothing so much as a blindfolded man who was staggering around trying to come in contact with some reality. But most of all, to establish contact with his wife. There was no question that he loved Melitta—and needed her.

They had both been hoping that when he had been off drugs for a meaningful period of time, they would be able to pick up their life as it was before. But it just was not working that way. They were miserable. He was lonely. And he was scared.

They played the Train Game in a straightforward Dominant-Submissive pattern. Melitta was the Dominant, something one might have predicted on two counts —first, because this is the historical stance of a black woman, and second, because Josh was an addict.

Melitta had played a very competent Dominant game, although as she said in the postgame session, "I didn't bother to listen to the instructions."

"Why not?" I asked.

"Well, I figured that's the man's job. Let him listen and tell me how to do it."

This, in a nutshell, was exactly how she ran their marriage. Her way of managing was invariably to say, "Let Josh do it." She rationalized this high-handed assigning of tasks by saying that if she acted "helpless," it would encourage Josh to be stronger. Actually, she was about as helpless as a cobra. And Josh knew it. He knew she would make him do everything—whether it was listening to the instructions, choosing a television program, or taking his son to the park. He realized that he was being forced to do things, that he was submitting to his wife's commands. There was no strength for him to be gained in this way.

I explained the significance of the Dominant-Submissive pattern in our postgame session and suggested to Melitta that if she would make an effort to be somewhat less aggressive, this would leave room on the scale of their interaction for Josh to become more aggressive, more of a man. She considered this thoughtfully but made no reply. Josh nodded as if he could immediately visualize the desirability of having a little more emotional elbow room. We worked along these lines for several months. Melitta tried hard to ease up a little and actually succeeded in becoming less rigidly moralistic about Josh's former drug addiction. And at that point it was former. He had been off drugs for six months before coming to me and had not slipped back during the subsequent five months of treatment.

A few months after they had begun treatment, the two of them came in obviously very disturbed. Melitta had found an old diary Josh had kept before they were married in which he had written in some detail about different women he had dated, including Melitta, and this infuriated her. It was distressing to be confronted with the fact that she had not been the one and only dominant woman in his life.

"But you were," I reminded her. "After all, you are the one he chose."

This brought on another outburst, one that revealed what was really bothering her. Josh had not only written about the women he went out with, but had written that he had decided to marry Melitta, because "I know she will push me to succeed." This had done it. Josh's acceptance of her power had upset Melitta more than anything. But as we discussed it, she acknowledged that she was not as upset as she would have been a couple of months earlier. Now she was able to be philosophical about the aggressive role assigned to the black woman since slavery days. But she claimed that she, for one, no longer wanted this role and she had been trying so hard to relinquish the reins in marriage over the past few months that the discovery of Josh's diary seemed like a betrayal.

At this point, Josh began asserting himself. He comforted Melitta, told her that she was more attractive and sexier than any of the other girls he had known—and that she shouldn't take his "bullshitting" to his diary so seriously. She laughed and told him to stop using that kind of language.

The session had marked a real step ahead for them. In the following weeks, it was obvious that they were beginning to feel closer and warmer to each other than they had for years. But at this point, just as it seemed that they were bringing about a change in their interaction, they stopped therapy. This was hardly surprising. While this happens with so many Dominant-Submissive couples, my experience with blacks, limited as it has been, suggests that they resist change even more strenuously than other Dominant-Submissives.

Could any professional have advised Melitta and Josh before marriage so that they could have avoided the pitfalls that led to addiction and to the lopsided power structure in their marriage? Hard to say. One could certainly have outlined the strengths and weaknesses of the Dominant-Submissive relationship. One might have advised Melitta that if she could manage to restrain herself from assuming total control, her husband would be able to be "more of a man" and play a more positive role within the pair. I suspect, however, that the correct treatment in these cases should probably start long before courtship and marriage. This interaction is undoubtedly instilled in childhood, possibly in infancy, as the black child is taught his or her sexual role.

14

Dominant-Submissive: The Masturbation Route

There is a great deal of sexual symbolism in the way pairs play the Train Game, symbolism that often provides the key that decodes part of the inner relationship. Some of it is rather superficial. A player will say, "I'll push your button," or "Wait until I tell you to move so we can come together," or "I'm really going to screw you this time."

The most overtly sexual play is seen in the variation of the Dominant-Submissive pattern that I call the Masturbation Route. One or both players takes the Alternate Route. One player proceeds right along the track to the finish. The other player goes along until he has almost reached the end—then he backs up! Then he goes forward again. And back and forth, back and forth with no seeming reason for the maneuver until finally he feels ready to finish the trip and proceeds to the end.

This pointless, compulsive self-pleasuring is always a sign of pathology—sometimes a clue to the fact that some minimal brain damage exists. One successful executive who exhibited this pattern reported that he had often been plagued by stupid little mistakes. When he described the mistakes, they were not so little. He often had difficulty when his wife would ask him to turn something on the stove off or on, when someone would give him directions when he was driving to veer to the left or right. He also would reverse his signature occasionally. Instead of signing "John Paulson," he would sign "Paul Johnson." Diagnostic tests revealed some brain damage, probably as a result of a bout with meningitis when he was in his mid-twenties.

The pathology more often is psychological. I remember one extremely intelligent couple, both gifted mathematicians, whose Train Game pattern was the Masturbation Route. I'll call them Tom and Claudia Pullan. Both started on the Direct Route. There was a collision. Claudia stood still. Tom reversed and took the Alternate Route. Claudia then continued to the finish point, while Tom simply ran his train back and forth on the Alternate Route. Finally he finished. It was as if he were giving a solo performance. He was not playing with his wife. He was playing with himself—masturbating.

In the postgame session, I asked Tom why he had played this way. "I was just doing my own thing," he said. "Enjoying myself."

This turned out to be the story of the marriage. Tom was not at all interested in what went on with Claudia. He was completely wrapped up in his own doings and feelings. He also liked to make things hard for himself. He had, for example, refused to buy a house until he could pay for it in one lump cash sum. The result was that they had been scrimping and saving for ten years, but had not yet been able to amass enough money to buy a house for cash. And at the same time, their standard of living had been very depressed because they tried so hard to put money aside for the house.

Another instance of delaying a final outcome was a research project that had engaged Tom at the university for the past five years. It was very complicated, and the results would be extremely important. But it would probably take another five years for Tom to come up with the final results because he refused to use the computer to speed up his work. He insisted that he himself do everything—even the most tedious, basic calculations.

As this all came out in the course of therapy, Claudia began to understand that Tom was solely involved with himself, that she could not depend upon him as a husband or even as a friend. This realization triggered Claudia's release, not from the marriage—she never considered separation or divorce—but from the one-sided, unfulfilled nature of the relationship.

One day she said, "That's just the way Tom is, isn't it? It's not my fault. And it's not his fault. That's just the way he is."

Once she understood that, she found herself other emotional supports. She switched from research to teaching, where she had daily interaction with the inquiring minds of her students. She became involved with the administration of the math department of the university, which provided her with another set of meaningful interactions. She did not do what one might have expected —find a lover. "I love Tom," she told me. Another instance of the strength of the Dominant-Submissive bond.

It is hard to understand why she loves and needs this man, but she does. Tom is unchanged. But the marriage interaction has changed. The stress has been significantly lessened. They are both more at ease. Claudia has been able to find the response Tom cannot give her through her work. This change was evidently enough to allow her to exist happily in the relationship. Once she realized that her husband was completely wrapped up in himself and always would be, this was all that was necessary.

In another case of the Masturbation Route variation, it was again the man who showed the back-and-forth, self-absorbed pattern. This was a less-educated couple, but the wife grasped the meaning of the masturbatory pattern as rapidly as Claudia had. Her way of coping was to experience a religious conversion.

A few weeks after she and her husband had played the Train Game, she came in and told me that she had "found God." On a sudden whim, she said, she had walked into a church, knelt down to pray, and suddenly felt that God was in her.

What she was really saying was, "It is impossible for me to comprehend what my husband is doing, but I cannot leave him. I need him. So I have found an alternative to depending on my husband. Now I will depend on God."

In both these cases—and they are typical—the sexual relationship was unsatisfactory. The man was more interested in his pleasure than in his wife's. Both women reported that they seldom experienced orgasm. But neither woman had any extramarital interests, and once they had understood their husbands' inability to be involved with them, this seemed to give them the ability to cope with the problems of the marriage in a constructive manner.

If one spotted this pattern in a couple on the verge of marriage, what could—or should—a therapist advise? I would advise, first of all, that such a couple decide not to have children. A marriage in which one partner is totally self-absorbed cannot provide a healthy environment for a child. The children of such a marriage would grow up with a pathological psychological and sexual warp. There could be, for instance, a predisposition to homosexuality or other sexual pathology.

Having said this, I would ask the woman if she could face the consequences of denying her biological urge toward motherhood. I would ask both to consult and consider what substitutes for children they could introduce into their lives. It is possible to compensate by, for instance, deep involvement with the older generation of the family or with nieces and nephews. In Claudia's case, she found herself a "family" of students. Some people find a dog is a satisfactory enough substitute. Others turn to creative endeavors—writing, painting, music, cooking, needlework, whatever.

I would also outline the implications of this pattern so that both partners understood the structure of the interaction. I would ask them to think carefully and deeply whether they could adapt their lives to this. Could the nonmasturbatory partner find the necessary response outside marriage without destroying the relationship? It may be that the ideal shift in the focus of interaction in this pattern would be a triangular relationship (the "nonmasturbatory" partner acquiring a lover and/or entering into some other close personal relationship), but that is pure speculation at this point.

15

Dominant-Submissive: Unhappily Ever After

The amount of punishment meted out to—and accepted by—the Submissive partner in a Dominant-Submissive relationship can be truly astonishing, especially in those unions that resist any change, no matter how slight.

I remember one such case. The husband, referred by his priest, came to see me first. He had beaten his wife several times, and she had gone home to her mother. Now, he said, he would do anything, anything, if she would only come back to him. He kept repeating that he would give "anything" to make peace with her.

"Why did you beat her up?" I wanted to know. "What set you off each time?"

It turned out that Rita and Mike had been going together ever since high school. They had intercourse almost from the beginning and she had gotten pregnant while still a junior in high school, and that scared Mike so much that he dropped her. Even when he heard that she had had a miscarriage, he never went to see her.

Mike graduated, went off to college, and four years later came home, got a job and started going out with

Rita once more. But now he was obsessed with the idea that she had had intercourse with other men in the five-year hiatus in their relationship. He kept asking her about the men she had dated and how far she had gone with them. He couldn't stay off the subject. It was like picking at a scab that itches, knowing that if one succeeds in picking the scab off, the wound will bleed again and hurt.

Rita felt that Mike had left her in the lurch when she was pregnant and it was none of his business what she had done in those five years. Nevertheless, she tried to placate him by answering his questions. Her answers never satisfied him. Despite this, they got married within a few months. When Mike came to see me, they had been married nine years and had four children—and Mike was still cross-examining Rita about the men she had known all those years ago. It was like having a resident district attorney in the household and being the resident culprit who continually had to testify against herself. Whenever Mike caught Rita in a contradiction, he would give her verbal hell. When he really got himself worked up, he would beat her.

I suggested that Mike concentrate on controlling himself if he wanted his wife back. He agreed. And Rita returned home with the children.

They started treatment together by playing the Train Game. Their interaction tested out as straight Dominant-Submissive. Mike was the Dominant. It was impossible to introduce any change into their relationship. During the five months they were in treatment, Rita went home twice again to her mother; each time she returned to Mike after a few days.

Her life was one long punishment, but it proved impossible to change the intensity of their interaction. They were united by this pathological "district attorney/criminal" relationship. Neither was willing, or, more accurately, neither was *able*, to change. They have now been married twelve years, are still miserable, and there is every likelihood that they will continue to live unhappily ever after.

Could one have predicted this outcome? Absolutely. The interaction revealed by the Train Game was unmistakable. Could one have alleviated some of this misery? I doubt it. The bond is so strong that no amount of physical and emotional trauma has been able to weaken it. So one could not expect a calm, rational explanation of the hazards of such a marriage to have affected their actions. The very fact that the bond survived five years of separation and neglect is testimony to the intensity of this particular Dominant-Submissive fusion.

16

Dominant-Submissive: Successful Separations

Although it is difficult to engineer a shift in the Dominant-Submissive interaction, it is not impossible, and there are some cases that I look back on with great satisfaction.

One dates from my earliest days in psychiatry—a lawyer and his wife. Joyce O'Neill, a pretty and intelligent woman, was a college English instructor. During the six years of her marriage to David, she had had a history of cyclical depressions, so severe that she would be admitted to the hospital. After two or three weeks, she would be back to "normal" and ready to go home. Everything would be fine until the next time. When the O'Neills came to me, Joyce's depressions were recurring about every five or six months. The immediate cause for their seeking therapy, however, was that David O'Neill had been having an affair with a woman who lived in the same apartment house they did, and Joyce had found out about it.

Very shortly after they came to me, Joyce went into a depression. In a couple of weeks, she was better and ready to leave the hospital. But I intervened. I said, "Absolutely not. Joyce is not ready to go home." I convinced husband and wife that it was time to break the cycle. Joyce could not go on for the rest of her life having to be hospitalized at ever-decreasing intervals. It was time to treat the depression.

The upshot was that Joyce stayed in the hospital for nine months. She was carefully supervised, and there were no serious depressive episodes during this period. Finally it seemed that since the five- to six-month cycle had been broken, at least for this once, Joyce could go home. But it turned out she was not sure she wanted to. She had had time to assess her life and had decided she wanted a divorce. This was discussed at length. David agreed to it, and divorce proceedings were initiated.

That was some years ago. Joyce has not had to go back to the hospital since. She has not remarried, but enjoys her teaching, has completed the work for a doctor's degree, and has a generally satisfying life.

Dave got remarried a couple of years after the divorce, but not to his mistress. He married someone very much like Joyce, and this marriage seems to have worked out well.

This, to me, was a successful outcome. The Dominant-Submissive couple was split, and each member of that original nuclear pair is better off for the separation. But the split was not easy. It required my intervention plus hospitalization and fairly effective isolation of Joyce from her husband for a significant length of time.

If I had not intervened so decisively, one could predict that Dave and Joyce would probably still be unhappily married, and Joyce would undoubtedly have entered an accelerated cycle of depressive episodes. So the intervention was worth the risk. But when I see that a patient needs help to make a change, I have no desire to subject him (or her) to the lengthy self-searching of traditional Freudian practice if I can nudge him onto a better track and save months, perhaps years, of unnecessary suffering. I do not agree with those therapists who consider this a dangerous shortcut. My experience is that people are so tough that—even in moments of psychic despair —they will instinctively resist any push in a destructive direction.

It also took an intervention on my part to help another Dominant-Submissive couple to a definitive separation. They came to me after they had been separated for a year. This was just one of many separations during the eleven years of their marriage. Their relationship resembled a game of table tennis more than a marriage; they bounced from separation to togetherness, back and forth, back and forth. It was as if some primitive, instinctual wisdom kept pushing them apart, telling them that they were a bad combination and quite destructive to each other, but the Dominant-Submissive bond was so strong that it kept yanking them back together again.

My intervention with this couple took the form of insisting that they continue their separation. I was not sure that they would be able to do it, but the shock of my intervention, the increasing self-knowledge stemming from my analysis of their interaction as revealed by the Train Game and the ensuing therapy sessions helped them to decide to make the separation permanent.

It was important to provide them with counseling and emotional support through the divorce period, especially the wife. She had been very childlike and unsure of herself. But almost from the moment that I prescribed a permanent separation, she began to mature and to think for herself. I was particularly impressed by one aspect of her new maturity. She had been very attached to her in-laws. And she managed to maintain that attachment through the divorce period and during the subsequent years, for her own sake and for that of the two children —an admirable achievement. It was difficult at the beginning, since feelings about the divorce ran high. But she persisted and succeeded in assuring her children of continuing warm relations with their grandparents.

One would never have believed that the immature woman who came to me bewildered by the pattern of separations during her marriage could have developed this strength, but once out of the destructive marital relationship, she was able to grow.

If I had been consulted early on, I would have given a bleak forecast for the future of these two marriages. Each of these pairs would have been immeasurably better off without the other. After analyzing their computer printouts from the Train Game, I would not have hesitated for a moment to tell them that unless they developed a great deal of individual emotional flexibility, their marriages would be unhappy, destructive unions.

The question inevitably arises, "What real good would this accomplish? If they had weighed the risks and decided not to marry, would their second choices of mates have been any better?"

One can't really answer that question. But I suspect they would have been. In the case of Joyce and David, David's second marriage seems to have been very happy and rewarding. And although Joyce did not remarry, she is happier and leads a better life as a single person than she did when she was married. Her pathological symptoms have disappeared, and she is functioning successfully at her job and with her friends.

In the second case, it is harder to tell. The husband did not remarry and neither did the wife. But it is a fact that the wife became more of a person after the divorce. She was able to develop her potential once the cyclic separations and reunions with her husband stopped. When and if she does remarry, I suspect that she will not choose a man like her first husband, because she has matured so enormously, and that she will not accept the submissive role in a Dominant-Submissive interaction. But this, of course, is pure speculation.

It is difficult to assess the effect premarital counseling would have with Dominant-Submissives, because the bond is so strong. But I think that if couples were given an honest, factual, unemotional report on the interaction of their relationship, what pattern it was and what the characteristics of that pattern were, they could think concretely about it and talk about it together. For many couples, the closeness of the Dominant-Submissive interaction and the role of leader or follower are extremely appealing because they fill each individual's needs and fuse the two into a nuclear pair, a human atom. For others, to whom the future might seem restricted within the confines of this interaction, the opportunity would be there to think twice, to think deeply about whether they wanted to take this calculated risk.

17

Dominant-Submissive:
"Hit Me Again"

Dissolution or separation is by no means the only successful or desirable resolution of a Dominant-Submissive relationship so stressful that the pair seeks professional help. Often, just a slight shift in the focus of interaction is enough to enable the pair to function more flexibly. These shifts usually occur as the result of increased self-knowledge. When a couple begins to see just what is going on between them, they can often introduce the necessary distance at stress points.

In one such successful case, the Train Game played a decisive role in mirroring a pair's behavior and shifting the focus of interaction. There was a massive Flipflop in which the dominant partner became the submissive and then later added the Cooperative interaction to his marital repertoire. And the formerly submissive member of the pair not only learned to take the dominant role, but acquired Cooperative and Competitive modes of interaction as well. The ability to change distances and roles to modify stress is like having a well-equipped tool box so that one can deal with almost any eventuality that comes up, whether it's a repair job or new construction. It is immensely satisfying to a therapist to watch a nuclear couple acquire the tools necessary to improve their mutual lives.

The Frederickses did just this. They were in their fifties; Burton was obviously a tyrant and Caroline was his slave. Burton was always criticizing her. He told her how to keep house, what to order for dinner, how to deal with the children. He was pompous and self-righteous. "Caroline can't do anything on her own," he told me. "I have to tell her everything as if she were a child."

Caroline, quite understandably, was a bundle of nerves. She was always on the verge of flying apart. She would be explosive and sullenly withdrawn in turn. When Burton had finally reduced her to a state of almost complete helplessness, he took the initiative and insisted that she go see a psychiatrist. He had read the Modern Library collection of Freud's writings and felt he was an expert on psychiatry. He liked to discuss psychiatric theory with me as if to say, "You better watch your step, Doctor, because I know as much as you do." There was also another angle to his parade of psychiatric knowledge: He was presenting himself as the "healthy" partner and his wife as the "sick" one and trying hard to push himself into the position of cotherapist.

Their game pattern was very rigid (see pp. 116–17). There was absolutely no unexpected bit of fantasy. It was an undeviating, back-and-forth, alternating Cooperative pattern, but there was one giveaway detail about it. The zigzags began with the first and second trips; the first zigged, the second zagged. This is the tipoff to a phony Cooperative. When the pattern is established at the beginning, this otherwise typical Cooperative pattern must

X = Burton Fredericks ——————
O = Caroline Fredericks —·—·—

Barrier	Route & Order of Finish	Direction	INITIAL		LEARNING				
1	1	0							
2	1	0							
1	1	1							
2	1	1							
1	1	2							
2	1	2							
0	1	2							
0	1	0	O	X	O	X	O	X	O
0	1	1							
1	0	0							
2	0	0							
1	0	1							
2	0	1							
0	2	0	X	O	X	O	X	O	
0	2	1							X
1	2	0							
2	2	0							
1	2	1							
2	2	1							
1	2	2							
2	2	2							
0	2	2							
0	0	0							
0	0	1							
Collision(s)									*
Trip			1	2	3	4	5	6	7

From the Initial phase on, Burton's and Caroline's playing indicates a concealed Dominant-Submissive pattern. (For information on how to interpret
this diagram, please refer to p. 61.)

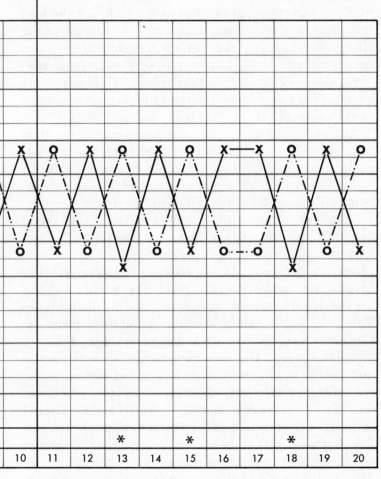

be accepted as a concealed Dominant-Submissive. The reason for this is that Cooperatives arrive at their zigzag pattern after a few exploratory trips, but the masquerading Dominant-Submissives start alternating from trip one, an indication that one of the players dictated the mode of play. One partner had to say, "I'll take the lead this time; you take it the next trip," in contrast to the Cooperatives, who, if they discuss their instinctive alternating pattern at all, usually phrase it something like, "Why don't we do such and such?" or "What do you say we try it this way?" Much different from issuing a command to the effect that "This is what you will do."

As I explained this in the postgame session, the Burtons seemed rather disconcerted. She was uneasy, because her husband had suddenly become copatient rather than cotherapist in her eyes. And he was angry at being dismissed from his self-designated role.

"The only thing you two cooperate in," I told them, "is creating extra stress between yourselves." They looked blank, and Burton proceeded with more complaints about his wife. He always had to clean up after her because she was so messy, he said. She left her makeup on the bathroom sink, magazines on the living-room floor, the dinner dishes were never put away properly. Caroline defended herself and made excuses for each "misdemeanor." This just gave him fresh ammunition and energy to cite more instances of her messiness.

Finally, I said sharply, "Burton, I heard you. She heard you. For God's sake, shut up!" And he did. Then I turned to Caroline and said, "You see. You can stop this flak, but you don't want to. You're just begging him to go on and on running you down. You play right into it. That's what I meant before when I said that the only way the two of you cooperated was to heighten the stress within the marital structure."

This got home to both of them. At that moment, they understood what they had just been doing. And from that time on, therapy seemed to progress well, so well that in several months I suggested that they might want to terminate for a while. They could always come back if the stress got too much for them, but they seemed to have learned how to stop their interminable back-and-forth of Burton's nagging and Caroline's submissive invitations to "hit me again while I'm down."

The change in interactions revealed by their "graduation day" play-through of the Train Game was truly staggering. This time Burton played a submissive game, in contrast to his previous dominant one. But even more amazing was Caroline, who seemed to enjoy exploring all the possibilities of the game. She tried to engage Burton competitively a few times, worked out a Cooperative pattern, and also assumed the dominant role. The extent of the learning that had taken place as revealed by the graph printout was amazing.

When we went over this change at the postgame session, Burton, the formerly nagging partner, burst into tears. I was perplexed. Had the change in interactions and roles upset him this much? I suggested that they continue in therapy until we worked this out.

At the next session, Burton, with great difficulty, blurted out that six years earlier he had begun an affair with another woman that lasted for several years. This had never come up before. Caroline was angry—and hurt. She rushed out of the room in tears. But she came back. They started talking to each other as they never had before. Suddenly, they were equals. Burton had stepped down off his pedestal. The confession had acted as an equalizer.

What had happened? What had made the change? Why had Burton confessed? It is all part of the dynamics of self-knowledge. They had been learning about themselves as individuals and as a nuclear pair. Caroline had been slowly gaining confidence in herself. One single change, Caroline's newly established confidence, had shifted the focus of interaction so that everything was different for Burton. The second play-through of the Train Game confirmed it: his falling into the submissive role, Caroline's almost gleeful experimenting with other patterns of interaction. Change had taken place. On top of that, nothing terrible had happened. The change that Dominant-Submissives resist so strenuously had taken place, and they were still together—and they felt better.

Now it was as if Burton's unconscious knew that it was not only safe but desirable to go ahead and confess. In a way, the admission was Burton's "present" to Caroline, whom he now viewed quite differently. She was no longer an inferior, an incompetent. She was an equal. And his present, the confession that he was less than perfect, introduced the missing piece into their relationship—reality.

Up to now, they had been acting, both of them, from mistaken perceptions. Caroline thought Burton was all-powerful; Burton thought Caroline was a nincompoop. Now they knew differently, and they were delighted. Reality can be frightening, but they were able to cope with it. They were able to discontinue therapy very shortly after this breakthrough. And they reported recently that all was well between them.

And without the reality that was reflected for them in

the second playing of the Train Game, I suspect that this couple would have been back for more therapy within very short order.

What about this one? Could an early diagnosis by the Train Game have prevented the miserable years of this marriage? It's hard to tell, but one can be optimistic and think that if Caroline could have been convinced that she was an intelligent, worthwhile person in her own right and that she should stand up to Burton's domineering, well . . . who knows? I like to think that it would have made a difference. The real question is, How much of a difference?

We don't know enough today to answer that question. But it will not remain unanswerable forever.

18

Cooperative: The Deceptive Ideal

Cooperative, working together toward a common goal—this is the ideal marriage. Or rather, it is what we are taught to consider ideal. The Cooperative pattern of interaction, which exists in about 15 percent of all marriages, would seem to be the best of all possible patterns in this imperfect world. In its purest version, each partner is allowed to follow his own ideas and inclinations, secure in the knowledge that both partners are striving toward the common goal. If there should be any disagreement on the best way to reach that goal, the partners alternate in an "After you, Alphonse," "After you, Gaston" courteous minuet.

How civilized! Ah, yes. And how dull!

Fairness, forbearance, consideration, understanding, loving mutuality, harmony—all these copybook virtues are unfortunately liable to add up to utter ennui when embodied in the Cooperative pattern of marital interaction. Cooperatives make good friends, but as mates—well, sometimes the truth is rather disillusioning.

There is far more extramarital adventuring among the

Cooperatives than among any of the other interaction patterns, partly because after a time the action between the home bed sheets is just too predictable. And so is the interaction in the rest of their lives. But philandering is not the reef these marriages usually split up on. More often they tend to expire of boredom.

Cooperation is one of those overrated virtues. A little goes a long way; too much may encourage boredom, infidelity—and divorce. An overdose of goodness is just too dull. Parents tell children to be good so that they can control them. That is a Dominant-Submissive relationship, but when the Submissive offspring get together, these goody-goodies form a Cooperative relationship and the result is often like lukewarm, unsalted soup.

Phonies tend to play the Train Game in a cooperative way because they don't want people to discover what they are really like. Other, more highly principled people may also play in a cooperative way that does not truly represent their true interaction, because they feel that they "should," that it is the "right" thing to do, the safe thing. And while this is not their "true" interaction, it does reflect honestly the way they conduct their relationships with others. They are not able to be themselves.

I remember one fascinating example of this, at a seminar on interactional behavior. Four Train Games had been set up in order to give all the counselors and therapists a chance to play. Each one played a game that tested out to the Cooperative pattern.

An observer, a computer expert who was more interested in how the data from the game was computerized than in how this group of therapists played, wanted more variety. He closed the barrier in one game after another, hoping that this might change some of the games to

Competitive or Dominant-Submissive. The players reacted with consternation. They absolutely rejected this uncooperative kind of play. In each case, the players opened the barrier and continued their carefully alternating play, as if to say, "We won't have any of this. We're going to cooperate, because we're civilized, well-balanced people."

This was both a self-protective mode of interaction and a conforming mode; it reflected their conception of how therapists should interact. Another self-protective mode of group interaction—in this case a group of intensely competitive businessmen—is described in Chapter 25, "Competitive: The 'Killer' Relationship."

Even the happiest husbands and wives, those couples who flourish in this interaction—and there are many, far more than those who seek psychiatric help or legal relief —tend to be the traditionalists of contemporary matrimony, finding quiet satisfaction rather than adventure in their marriages and in each other. They glory in their unexceptionality.

Often these couples are extremely successful in the business world or socially. Their complete, taken-for-granted cooperation makes them a formidable team. And there are times when complete cooperation can have exhilarating results. I like to draw an analogy with sports. The coxswain of a college crew calls out the stroke and steers the boat. It is exhilarating when the boat "sets up" and everyone is working in unison, perfectly coordinated, perfectly cooperating. Then the boat seems to glide. One doesn't feel anything. But this lasts only for very brief periods. No crew can sustain it for any significant length of time. Some crews never achieve it. But it is a wonderful feeling while it is happening.

When a nuclear pair can achieve that kind of cooperation and it is directed toward a goal, it can be equally exciting. This is the other side of the coin from the prosaic, everyday, commonplace cooperation. This high level is hard to maintain, but it is a goal for the cooperatively interacting pair and can add some of the spice that these marriages often lack. The Cooperatives do not overload the marital system the way the Dominant-Submissives do. When they do have trouble, it is because there is not enough electricity racing back and forth between the partners.

The Cooperative graph yielded up by the Train Game is as individual and easy to recognize as the Dominant-Submissive one. It is a series of interlocking zigzags that may be haphazard at the beginning but after the fourth or fifth trip, the zigs usually begin to approximate the zags, as in the graph on pages 126–7.*

Although the Cooperative pattern may be as stifling in its lack of excitement as the Dominant-Submissive is in its rigid lockstep, I consider it a less primitive pattern, a commitment to working together. In the Train Game,

*If the zigs and zags attain equality from the very beginning, this is a clue that the interaction shown is not a true Cooperative pattern, but rather a Sneaky Dominant-Submissive. To establish equality from the first trip, one partner has to have indicated, "We are going to cooperate," and the other submissively followed his lead. Then what we have is a rather frenetic series of Flipflops, each lasting for only one or two trips. While there is a strong element of Cooperative here, the initial, underlying interaction is that old primitive Dominant-Submissive. Depending on the strength of the various interactions, I categorize these couples as Dominant-Submissive or as a hybrid variety that belongs to the Minor Four patterns, a Dominant-Submissive/Cooperative, which I shall describe in Chapter 31.

X = Husband ————————
O = Wife —·——·——·——·

Barrier	Route & Order of Finish	Direction	1	2	3	4	5	6	7
1	1	0						O	
2	1	0							
1	1	1							
2	1	1							
1	1	2							
2	1	2							
0	1	2							
0	1	0	O	X	X	O		X	O
0	1	1							
1	0	0	X						
2	0	0							
1	0	1							
2	0	1							
0	2	0			O	X		X	
0	2	1						O	
1	2	0							
2	2	0							
1	2	1							
2	2	1					X		
1	2	2							
2	2	2							
0	2	2							
0	0	0		O					
0	0	1							
		Collision(s)						*	
		Trip	1	2	3	4	5	6	7

INITIAL · LEARNING

During the Resolution phase, the husband and wife show an alternating Cooperative pattern of interaction, with the only collision(s) occurring on Trip 14. (For information on how to interpret this diagram, please refer to p. 61.)

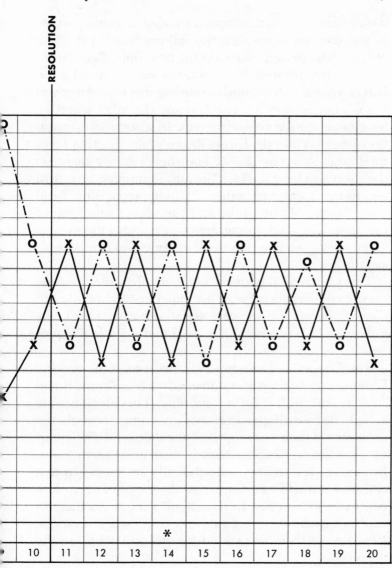

the commitment is manifested by allowing one partner to win the first game with the full expectation that the other will be permitted to win the next time. Reciprocity is taken for granted. Cooperatives may each take the Direct Route, with the understanding that one player will make a larger score on one trip and the other will have his chance on the following trip. In a significant variation, one may take the Direct Route while the other takes the longer Alternate Route and they will take turns on the short and long tracks. This variation reflects a lack of involvement with each other, a psychic separation. I call it the Divorce Route. Julie and Jim played one form of this variation. They cooperated—or perhaps the word is "connived"—so that they seldom came into contact with each other.

This paradoxical pattern, which involves the most exquisite cooperation, has in my experience always led to divorce, except for one very significant case, which may indicate a breakthrough in marital therapy (see Chapter 22).

The Cooperatives do not resist treatment the way the Dominant-Submissives do. Instead, they welcome it and tend to stick with it for a long time. They demonstrate a high degree of perseverance in going through the problems of their marriage with the therapist. The greatest problem in treating them is their great fear of confrontation. Just as they automatically back away from a collision in the Train Game, so they avoid face-to-face confrontations in life. In treatment, I try to get them to confront each other, to fight, to let out their grievances. I encourage them to make decisions and act upon the decisions.

The utter predictability of these unions is their downfall. I do not know why some Cooperatives live together in humdrum bliss and why others flee from it. But if I were to advise Cooperatives before they embarked on marriage or some other form of mutual commitment, I would tell them to guard against too much "niceness," and never, never to pussyfoot around the problems and disagreements that must arise in any marriage. That little spark of extra electricity generated by the heated interaction needed to settle their marital conflicts may be just what's needed to counteract the "good scout" aspects of these unions.

19

Cooperative:
Scared—Almost to Death

Many couples who test out to the Cooperative pattern are scared to death. Scared of decisions, confrontations, disagreements, scared of each other, and of losing each other.

They are not, however, frightened of change the way the Dominant-Submissives are. And they are not afraid to explore their relationship or to work to change it. I am always amazed at how long and at what psychiatric depth these couples are willing to work with me and each other to improve their relationship. As they slowly clear away all the minor entanglements and misunderstandings (I think of these as emotional underbrush), there is always one enormous problem left—fear. Often this is the first time they have recognized it, because it has been hidden by all that "underbrush."

Finally, there it is—naked fear. What is it they are afraid of? And why do they dare not confront their fear?

Erica and Lucien Levy were a typical pair of Cooperative interactors. And their whole married life—eight years of it—had been shadowed by fear, fear of which they had been absolutely unconscious.

Erica worked on a fashion magazine. Lucien was in advertising. They had agreed before they got married that they would not have a child until they were ready financially. They had never discussed their emotional readiness, or even considered it. Now, after eight years, Erica wanted a child desperately. But she never told Lucien. She never came out and said, "I would like to have a baby. I think the time has come for us to start a family." Once in a while she would say something like, "When we have a baby, we'll have to get a larger apartment," or, "When we have a baby, perhaps we should move to the suburbs." She felt that this was raising the subject, putting it on the table for discussion. But she never pursued it beyond these very tentative remarks.

Nor did Lucien pick up these cues. He was conscious only in the most peripheral way that his wife had said something about having a baby. He hadn't really listened. He didn't want to hear.

Then suddenly, one February morning in the predawn hours, Erica made a suicide attempt. Lucien found her slumped on the bathroom floor, an empty bottle of sleeping pills beside her—found her in time.

Lucien was bewildered. He had no idea what had set her off, no idea that she was miserable. Their life, it seemed to him, had been harmonious, a little dull, but agreeable on the whole and certainly much more pleasant than the lives of some of their married friends. Lucien had had a couple of unimportant—and rather disappointing—love affairs, but he considered that he had never been emotionally unfaithful to his wife.

Now the Levys were trying to find out what had gone wrong with their marriage.

"I didn't know she wanted a baby so much," Lucien told me.

"But you knew she wanted one," I said.

"Well . . ." and his voice faded off.

"What about you?" I asked. "Did you ever think about having a child? A son? Or what it would be like to have a daughter?"

"Yes, sometimes. But not right now. It would tie us down too much."

It became evident that Lucien was aware of Erica's desire for a baby, but since he wasn't ready to settle down and didn't want the added responsibility of a child, he avoided the subject. So it hung there between them —until Erica forced a confrontation by her suicide attempt.

Erica and Lucien tested out as a true Cooperative pattern. In the Train Game, they conscientiously made certain that each came out even, and they evaded, ducked, skirted the very idea of colliding or using the barriers. They were like two boxers in a ring, neither of whom dared lay a glove on the other.

In the postgame session, I pointed out how closely their play duplicated their handling of Erica's desire for a child—and Lucien's unwillingness to have one. It turned out that this was the way they handled all problems, large or small, that arose in their lives. They excitedly told me of one incident that could have been the model for everything they did. They decided to buy a car. Each secretly wanted a foreign sports car, but neither said so because of the expense. After a certain amount of discussion they bought a Volkswagen, a sensible enough choice, but still and all, not the car that either of them wanted.

"Why didn't you tell each other that you were dying to have that ten-thousand-dollar sports car? What would have happened if you'd said so?" I asked.

They looked at each other. Lucien laughed. "I suppose we now would be the proud owners of a ten-thousand-dollar sports car."

"With a racing-green finish," Erica added wistfully.

"And how about if you had been able to talk about starting a family?" I asked.

Silence.

Then Lucien said, "Erica wouldn't have had to take all those pills, I suppose."

Erica cried. When she was able to talk, she looked at me and said, "I know. Perhaps we would be the proud parents of a beautiful child. That's what you mean, isn't it?"

If they could not level with each other about an automobile, how could they express their feelings about having a baby? Lucien had been impervious to all of Erica's many hints because he did not dare talk about his fears that a baby would change their life, his horror at the idea of being tied down. Nor could Erica explain how she felt the years were passing faster and faster and soon it might be too late to start a family.

They were frightened of losing each other's love, so each bent over backward to avoid confrontations. As therapy continued, they came to understand this very clearly. And one day they came in absolutely glowing to report an important breakthrough. They had had a fight! Lucien had become so angry he had pounded the kitchen table and broken it. It was a pleasure to observe their delight in having dared to fight this marital battle only to find that nothing terrible happened. It was a giant step for them in understanding that they could confront each other without destroying the relationship.

As time went on, conflict solving was no longer such a hazard. And with their new flexibility, they discovered a new fascination with each other. There was more spark in the marriage.

The time came when they were ready to discuss starting a family. As it turned out, there was very little to discuss. Erica still wanted a baby. And Lucien had come to look forward to being a father. Then there was a setback. Months went by and Erica had not conceived. After a series of tests, it turned out that she was not able to have children.

It was a heavy blow, but Erica weathered it. A few months later, they decided—and it was a mutual decision —to adopt a baby. That was two years ago. They are now looking for a second child to adopt. Their lives have changed tremendously. They have learned to work as a team, without fear that conflict or disagreements will hinder the relationship. Their new openness has taught them that their old fears were largely unjustified.

What could I have done to help Lucien and Erica if they had come to me during their courtship? I would have encouraged them to learn how to fight. The typical fight-phobic relationship of the Cooperatives would have been clearly delineated in the graph depicting their interaction during the Train Game. Learning how to acknowledge conflicts and resolve them could have changed their married life—probably quite dramatically. The ability to deal with different needs would have forestalled such a desperate statement as Erica's suicide attempt. In essence, this nearly fatal gesture was the only way she was able to tell Lucien that she wanted a baby —and that she knew he did not.

But could they really have been taught to disagree openly and work out their disagreements? Probably. My prescription would have been simple enough: a rough, tough engagement. Instead of blissfully sailing through the engagement period and allowing such matters as how many people should be invited to the wedding, where the reception would be held, and all the other "weighty" decisions a wedding involves to be settled by their respective parents, as usually happens, I would have advised them to decide exactly what they wanted—and fight for it. If it turned out that Erica wanted six bridesmaids and two hundred wedding guests and Lucien wanted to be married in City Hall, they should have fought it out themselves—as well as where to spend the honeymoon, another great battleground. If she wanted Bermuda and he Tahiti, they should have worked it out to a mutually agreeable solution.[18]

The benefits of this early fight training would have been enormous. They would have learned that the sky would not fall in when they had a fight. And they would have been able to start their married life with a minimum of that fear that bedevils most Cooperatives—at least, those Cooperatives who end up in a psychiatrist's office.

20

Cooperative:
Folie à Deux

Folie à deux, a psychiatric term used to describe a kind of mutual delusion, is the name I give to a variation of the Cooperative pattern in which the partners agree to believe something that is contrary to fact. One partner latches on to some mad idea and the other falls in with it. In the Train Game, it usually takes the form of one player deciding that the tester is rigging things. The problem they are having, he explains to his partner, is caused by the tester—not the husband, not the wife, but the tester. This erroneous idea becomes instant gospel.

This was the case with Max and Sally Kantor. Max was an overachiever, and he relished the rewards of his overachieving—his high income, his top-management position, even the hovering of headwaiters in expensive restaurants. All this represented more than the rewards of hard work; to Max, it represented love. His overachieving was spurred by a search for love. He had had a mistress for years, another evidence of his craving for love. His wife seemed to accept the liaison with equanimity.

Sally was just the opposite of her husband; she was an underachiever. She must have been quite attractive once, but when the Kantors came to see me, she was fat and sloppy. One indication of her lack of pride in her appearance was that she wore bedroom slippers to the first session. She had no interests outside the home, and took very little interest in her home now that the children were on their own.

The early days of their marriage had been externally difficult: They had had very little money, Max had had to travel a lot. And they had been very happy.

Then Max began to succeed, and everything else started going downhill. In his increasing absorption in his work, he withdrew more and more from Sally and the children. Sally's reaction was to do nothing. She took no steps to restructure or strengthen the marriage. She never confronted Max with her feelings of being neglected and alone. Nor did Max ever try to spur his wife into taking a more active part in his life.

Most successful men, rightly or wrongly, tend to feel that their wives are a reflection of themselves and their achievements. The wife, by her looks, her expensive clothes, her well-decorated house, confirms the husband's success. This was not true of Max. He accepted Sally as she was. He never criticized the way she let herself go, just as Sally never brought up the subject of Max's mistress. In most marriages when the wife discovers that her husband is involved with another woman, she fights tooth and nail to break it up—but not Sally.

Their lives, in short, had been faithfully reflected by the Train Game. Just as Max and Sally had jointly seized on the false idea that the tester was trying to cause difficulties for them, so they seized on the idea that someone else, some outside force, was responsible for their marital unhappiness. Each partner had cooperated in setting up an outside excuse for the breakdown of their marriage. There was Max's mistress. There was Max's job that required all his time and energy. There was Sally's apathy, which gave Max an excuse for ignoring her.

I explained to them that they had worked together to make a mess out of their marriage just as they had worked together in the Train Game to convince themselves that the tester was in control.

When they played the game, Max and Sally established a Cooperative pattern after the first few trips, but no matter how they tried, they could not avoid collisions. They played a smash-crash-bang game. Trip after trip, the red lights flashed as they collided. They could not understand why they kept colliding. Then Max came up with the "solution." Here is an excerpt from their taped running commentary:

MAX: We waste so much time with these fucking collisions. I don't know why we keep having them.

SALLY: There must be a way to avoid them.

MAX: Oh! Oh! I think I've got it. The collisions are not our fault. It's the tester. She controls the trains, don't you see? She's *making* us collide.

SALLY: How can she do that?

MAX: There's no problem. Don't you see? It's all electric. All she has to do is push some button and the red light flashes and the trains stop. I've got it all figured out. They want to find out how we react when the going gets tough.

With this false "insight," Max and Sally played on—each trip still a crash-bang affair—but now at each collision, Sally would say, "There she goes again. Messing up our game."

Both now acted as if they had nothing to do with what was going on in front of them, although they still maintained the Cooperative pattern and still collided. They started to call the tester the "cruise director." This was apt, since they were behaving as if they were on a luxury cruise where they never had to make a decision because everything was in the hands of the cruise director.[19]

It need not have worked out that way. Sally had come close to figuring out how to avoid a collision just before Max came up with his explanation of "it's the tester who makes us collide," but the moment Max put forth this illogical idea, Sally stopped thinking along her previous logical lines and fell in with Max's thinking.

I took the couple back to the testing room after reviewing all this with them. After emphasizing again that the tester had nothing to do with the results, I set them to replaying the game. And they collapsed. Now that they could not blame their problems on an outside agency, they fell apart. Their play became stupid and erratic. The Cooperative pattern disappeared, and their second game graphed out to the Chaotic pattern (see Chapter 34). It was a very traumatic confrontation with themselves.

The trauma pervaded every area of their mutual lives, they told me at the next session. They had been miserable all week, shaky, unsure of themselves. Their distress —and it was very real—was caused by the dramatic and traumatic shift in the focus of interaction between husband and wife. Now, instead of agreeing that everything rotten in their lives was the fault of some outside person or force, they had to face the fact that their problems were of their own making. This was not easy. To make a shift like this in the course of a single hour as they had is as life-shaking as getting married or divorced or having a baby. I liken the nuclear couple engaged in shifting their focus of interaction to a house that is being completely remodeled. The shell remains the same, but the interior structure has to be gutted before a new and better structure can be built.

The trauma of this "remodeling" was relatively short-lived. It did not take more than a few weeks for the Kantors to adjust and experiment with more constructive patterns of interaction. It was as if they had said to themselves, "All right, if this is the way things really are, then this is what we had better do." And they had done it. This quick switchover is typical of the *folie à deux* variation.

What was it they had done? Basically they had accepted responsibility for themselves and no longer blamed outside "demons" for all of life's frustrations— by which they gave themselves a kind of "permission" not to try to do anything about their problems. Now that they knew they controlled their own lives, it seemed easier for them to take direct action.

Their whole pattern of interaction has changed. They are still Cooperatives, but where what they had shared before was a delusion (and delusions naturally stand in the way of effective interactions), now they share reality. Hard as it may seem to be, reality is much easier to cope with in the long run.

There have been no magic results. Sally has lost weight. But Max still has his mistress. Sally and Max have begun to change their lives in many ways. Max will always have an inordinate craving for love, but he is beginning to understand that giving love is the way to get love, that he can't buy it.

And they still have fits of *folie à deux* when one or the other will come up with some absolutely irrational idea. But now they are learning to be more cautious about accepting these crazy concepts. They have learned to think twice, to challenge the partner who proposes the newest madness. They have learned that such confrontations do not bring on disaster.

Could the kind of mutual craziness that crippled Max and Sally for so many years have been prevented if they had been diagnosed by the Train Game before marriage? The answer is yes—if the marriage could have been prevented. Or if one or the other or both had learned to control these runaway delusions. If I had been consulted, I would have presented the hazards in my most forceful manner so they would have been able to make an informed decision about getting married. And I believe any other counselor with adequate information would have done the same thing, because a *folie à deux* pairing is dangerous. It is a sick pattern; there is no built-in corrective for this mutual madness, no built-in system of checks and balances.

Folie à deux is the kind of magical thinking characteristic of early childhood, very similar to the infant's belief that his bottle appears because he cries. This magical thinking is normally relinquished as the child grows in experience and understanding. But Max and Sally still clung to their infantile beliefs.

The bond between these pairs, however, is so extremely strong that probably nothing I or any other adviser could have told them would have changed their minds about getting married. In any case, I would encourage them at least to postpone the marriage for a time, the longer the better, while both explored the sub-

ject further with professional help. During that time, I
would hope that one of two things would happen.

First, I would hope that either Max or Sally would
benefit enough from therapy to control this magical
thinking. In that case, I would not protest the marriage,
for, just as it takes two to tango, it takes two to set up a
folie à deux. As Selma Fraiberg puts it in discussing the
magical beliefs of children, "Whatever a magician be-
lieves, the truth of the matter is that he derives his power
from his audience. The career of a magician ends in the
moment that his audience disbelieves his magic."*

If one partner is strong enough to resist the delusions
of the other, that is enough—if Sally, for instance, had
said to Max, "What are you talking about? That's crazy.
The game is to test how we relate to each other, not to
the tester. That's obvious. And I bet we can work out a
way not to collide. Let's try . . ."

Second, I would hope that if the above did not happen,
either or both would be weaned away from the other.
The insights and maturity brought on by therapy could
be sufficient in some cases to make one or both members
of this pair realize, "That's not the man/woman for me."

*Selma Fraiberg, *The Magic Years* (New York: Charles Scribner's
Sons, 1959).

21

Cooperative:
The Divorce Route

Most couples whose Train Game pattern graphs out to the Divorce Route variation carry on their relationship by a kind of remote control. Although most insist they want to maintain their marriage, to improve it, and say they are willing to work at it (and they do work), they cannot get together again.

They play the game in the most distant way possible. One takes the Direct Route, the other the Alternate. And they alternate between the two. They do not experiment with ways they can beat the game. They can't collide. Distance is the message they send out. And they usually believe that this is the *only* way to play the game, the only possible way. There are slight variations within the pattern, of course, but this about sums up the interaction.

Julie and Jim were one such couple. Julie's recollection of how they played the game was reported in Chapter 3, "Destination: Divorce." They had been married for ten years. By their account, everything had been great for the first six. Then something happened. Neither knew just what, but the magic disappeared. Friction, dissatisfaction, misunderstandings made up the fabric of their life together. Jim became completely wrapped up in his work, putting in twelve to fourteen hours a day. Their sex life eroded. Julie became resentful at being left alone —and left responsible for running the house, paying the bills, taking care of vacation plans. "I might as well be single," she said. "As it is, all I am is an unpaid servant. I even pay my own way, because I have my own job."

But the more Julie did, the more Jim demanded. The more she indulged him, the more he wanted to be indulged, like an unhappy child who wants something but does not know what he wants or when to stop demanding. None of this giving and taking, however, brought them together. It had the effect of putting even more distance between them as Julie lost respect for a man who would ask so much and Jim began to look on Julie as an unobliging housekeeper rather than a wife.

Yet they were obviously fond of each other. Jim kept insisting that everything would be all right if there were more sex in the marriage. When they first saw me, Jim stated flatly that he was deprived of sex. "I'm sick and tired of masturbating," he shouted. Julie countered that the only time they had sex was when she made the advances. They both seemed sincere. There was either a great discrepancy of perceptions here—or of needs.

After they played the Train Game, it was easy to see that their case was nowhere near as simple as they had described it. Here was a straightforward Divorce Route game.

They were very earnest about working at their marriage, but it soon became clear that Julie was more uncomfortable in it than she was conscious of being. After one session in which she had endured a series of particularly brutal complaints and criticisms from Jim, many of them centering on her sexual deficiencies, I suggested that a trial separation might be in order. Julie accepted the idea without hesitation. Jim protested. He asserted that he would not move out. At that point, Julie, who felt Jim was not making enough money to be able to support himself, moved into the maid's room—an indication not only of her low self-esteem, but a kind of underlining of the position she felt she had in the household—servant.

They both, in the dogged manner of Cooperatives, continued therapy. We examined the basis of many of their feelings and emotions. Then, one morning, Julie clumsily dropped a light bulb. And this precipitated the divorce. Jim reacted to the noise with an exaggerated shudder and a shout. Sweeping up the fragments was a minute's work, but when it was over, Julie said, "Jim, let's separate before we hate each other so much that we'll never be able to be friends." He agreed. It was as simple as that.

Once separated, Jim demonstrated great strengths, proving himself able to set up his own apartment and manage his own life very capably. So did Julie. They were able to work out an amicable divorce and, after the initial trauma, have been able to maintain a relationship in which they enjoy seeing each other every few months. Neither has remarried, but both have established satisfactory social and sexual relationships with other people.

Therapy continued for several months after they separated. Each needed help to recognize his own strengths as an individual and to bolster those strengths.

Could one have predicted this divorce if Julie and Jim had played the Train Game before marriage? My answer today is, Yes. In the next chapter, however, I will discuss a case, the only such case I have had so far, where the Divorce Route has been "rerouted" to bypass a divorce. But except for this case, every other Divorce Route pattern I have seen has ended in divorce, despite heroic and imaginative therapy on my part and that of other colleagues who have treated couples showing this interaction.[20]

Should the marriage have been prevented? I do not think so. This is a question that is increasingly significant today in face of the escalating divorce rate. My feeling is that in this particular case and in some others I have treated, the rewards of the marriage outweighed its negative aspects and even the trauma and dislocations attendant on divorce and the starting of a new life. I believe that each individual comes out of these marriages with more strength and a heightened potential. The former nuclear pair tend to remember certain stages of their marriage as constructive and rewarding.

Would couples in this category have been better off simply having an affair rather than getting married? That is a rather old-fashioned question today. To my way of thinking, an affair between two individuals involves as much commitment as a marriage. There are social conveniences to marriage, of course, but even those are disappearing these days.

I might advise such a couple coming to me today that they would be as well off if they planned to live together without benefit of license or ceremony—if they are not planning to have children. And the only reason I would advise this is simply to avoid the expense of legal fees and the farce of the divorce ritual when the breakup finally comes.

If such a pair insisted that they wanted to have children, all I could do in that case would be to review the history of the Divorce Route couples I have treated and ask them what provisions they would make for their still unborn children in case of divorce. In the event that this consideration did not deter them, I would hope that by the time their Divorce Route brought them to the marriage counselor, I or some other therapist would have been able to break the inevitability of this pattern, have learned how to get this variation of the Cooperative pattern back on the married "happily enough" track.*

*For a more detailed discussion of the Divorce Route, see Robert A. Ravich, "The Marriage/Divorce Paradox," in Sager, C. J., and Kaplan, H. S., eds., *Progress in Group and Family Therapy* (New York: Brunner/Mazel, Inc., 1972).

22

Cooperative:
The Divorce
That Did *Not* Happen

The case that I hope will mark a turning point in treating those marriages that graph out as Divorce Route variations is that of the Hilbergs. John and Hazel Hilberg played an unmistakable divorce pattern, although at points it exhibited a tendency toward the Competitive.

I asked myself, "What in the world can I do to help this couple? Is there any way I can possibly turn this relationship around?" There is a terrible pitfall awaiting the unwary psychiatrist who treats a number of cases that fall into the same pattern and have the same outcome. He has to be constantly alert, to fight against accepting the pattern. The self-fulfilling prophecy is no myth. One has to treat every case with the expectation that this one will be different, that this one will not end in divorce or separation. Each time, I try to come up with some variation in therapy, some fresh insight, something, anything that will reverse the motion toward divorce.

Now here were the Hilbergs, intelligent, lively, good-looking. They had three children (two of them were married), and they were well-to-do. Why should they be in such straits that they had to ask for help with their marriage? Was there anything I had not tried with other couples that I could try with the Hilbergs?

In this case my answer was cotherapy. I had utilized this before, but not with Divorce Route pairs. Perhaps it would make the difference. I brought in a skilled woman therapist with whom I had worked on other cases. I did not show her the Hilbergs' game pattern, nor did I tell her that they had played the Divorce Route variation. I did not want the slightest shadow of a self-fulfilling prophecy to intrude on her attempts to help.

It turned out that the main issue dividing the family was the youngest daughter, Annika, sixteen. Annika was smoking pot and fooling around with "uppers" and "downers," running around with blacks and Puerto Ricans who were much older than she was, failing at school. She had had an abortion and told her parents she did not know who the father might have been. She was the outcast of this otherwise very proper family.

Hazel wanted to send Annika off to a very strict girls' school that specialized in problem girls. She would be carefully supervised, and there would be no opportunity for sexual escapades or experimentation with drugs.

John wanted to keep the girl at home. He said that the school was like a jail and would incite Annika to further rebellion. He felt she would straighten out "by herself."

It was obvious that the girl should be brought into the therapy sessions. Annika came in with her parents. I encouraged her to talk about the kind of life she was leading, and how she felt about her parents. She was very troubled and insecure, but obviously relieved to have a chance to talk about her feelings. She stated that her parents did not love her the way they loved her brother and sister, that they did not want her around, and that her mother actually hated her.

This was like a little atom bomb. Hazel was completely shaken. She could not believe that her daughter could feel this way. She insisted that her strictness showed her love.

Hazel was further shaken when her husband said he often felt the same way; he felt that his wife disapproved of him to the point of hatred when he wanted to do something she considered "wrong" or foolish. When he was pressed for instances, he cited some of his sexual fantasies that Hazel refused to go along with and his desire to take a six-month sabbatical so that he and Hazel could live in Florence—a dream he had always had.

It came out that John had had a mistress for several years who enjoyed the sexual fantasies that Hazel disapproved of and whom he had taken on many business trips that Hazel had refused to go on because she was too busy at home. Again Hazel was absolutely rocked. Rocked and shocked. She insisted that none of these things had ever come out as sources of conflict. John would suggest them, Hazel would indicate her disapproval, and that would be that—the typical avoidance of conflict seen in the Cooperative pattern and the ever-increasing distance typical of the Divorce variation. And it was Hazel obviously who had set the Divorce pattern. John had simply adjusted his life to her "rule" of "Let's keep plenty of distance between us."

But Annika's recital of her feelings brought all Hazel's and John's suppressed emotions to the surface. Now the cotherapist proved to be most useful. Our five-cornered sessions seemed to shift the interaction. More than that, neither had the excuse that the therapist did not understand because of being of the opposite sex. This was a distinct advantage in treatment, because we were able to keep the Hilbergs from retreating to their distant, noncombat positions. It was easier to insist that each issue be brought out in the open and discussed.

Hazel and John started getting into contact with each other, discussing substantive issues and letting the other know his or her real feelings. They no longer retreated. As their involvement with each other grew, the cotherapist and I diminished our roles, emerging only when a nudge of some sort seemed needed.

The immediate problem was solved rather promptly: Hazel and John agreed that Annika should stay at home. They also arranged for the girl to have therapy with a psychiatrist who was skilled in treating adolescents, and they agreed to participate in the therapy whenever the doctor requested it.

At one point, Hazel said, "I suppose we have Annika to thank for saving our marriage. She was the only thing left that really got to us, that we felt strongly about." And while this conclusion was somewhat of an exaggeration, it contained considerable truth.

The Hilbergs were in therapy for about a year and a half. By that time, Annika was doing much better and was talking about going to summer school so she would have a chance of getting into college the following year. The "inevitable" divorce did not take place. This does not mean that it never will, but I am optimistic about this marriage. It may be that in these cases, it takes both a male and female therapist to push the partners together enough for them to start relating to each other again.[21]

23

Cooperative:
The Abyss of Boredom

Another earmark of the Cooperatives is that they are afraid to have fun. When they play the Train Game, I always wonder why—once they have learned how to play in the most profitable manner for those imaginary penny payoffs—they then don't reconnoiter a little bit, experiment with other possibilities of the game and have a little fun. But they cannot seem to bring themselves to do it. They go back and forth in their nicely balanced pattern —zig and zag and zag and zig, seldom changing. It is boring, a kind of sterility. These people cannot have fun because they are so intent on doing things "right" or making the most money.

One couple I treated were terribly sunk in the abyss of boredom. Before marriage, Polly had been a very active person, involved in her job, in politics, intensely involved in the world of art. She was lively and had a lot of friends. Jerry married her knowing this—and loving it in her. And then, Polly retired from the world.

It started when her first child was born. It was a difficult pregnancy and it took her some time to feel vigorous again. Then their second child was on the way. The children were in the mid-teens when Polly and Jerry came to me. Polly complained that she was bored to death. Jerry never talked to her, never confided in her. "We never go any place or do anything," she said.

Jerry had the identical complaints. "Polly never has anything to say. She never wants to do anything. She's there when I come home from work at night, ready to drain me. She's like an inquisitor. She wants to know everything of interest I did during the day. Even what I had for lunch. And every night, I just have to tell her that it was a day like other days. Nothing much went on, and I had tuna fish on whole wheat for lunch with a cup of black coffee."

"What about it?" I asked Polly. "Don't you talk to your husband? Haven't you anything to tell him?"

"Well," she said after a little reflection, "I guess all I have to talk about is playing tennis and taking the dog to the vet and how expensive everything is at the supermarket."

So between his tuna fish sandwich and her reports on the supermarket, no wonder they were bored. But why had they let themselves fall into this? They were both intelligent. Jerry had a good job, a good income. It turned out that they never went to the theater, seldom went to the movies, never went to the art exhibitions that had once been Polly's great joy in life. In fact, Polly seldom ever went shopping for herself.

They had gotten to the point where they depended on their teen-age children to supply the conversation at the dinner table. The activities of the youngsters were the focal interest of their lives. But the youngsters were making their own lives, wanted to be with their own friends, and were involved in their own activities. After their dinner-table reports on school and sports, they retired to their rooms to do homework or telephone their friends. Polly and Jerry were left to their own boredom. And that of the television set until it was late enough for them to escape to bed. To bed, to sleep. Their sexual life had slowed down to a duty performance every week or so.

It seemed that this couple was dead set against—or scared of—having anything interesting in their lives. The problem was to introduce a little fun, some stimulation. After several sessions I asked Polly, "If you were free to do anything in the world, absolutely anything, what would you do?"

"Oh, I'd go back to work," she said promptly. This was surprising, because she had never indicated the slightest interest in this before. "I'd take some courses in design and try to get a job with a decorating firm," she continued. "I'm sure one would take me on a commission basis."

"What's stopping you?" I asked. "What are you frightened of?"

Polly could not come up with an answer, and it was obvious that she was very hesitant about committing herself to any course of action. Jerry stepped in and said, "You ought to do it. Why not? The kids can manage by themselves after school. They're never home until it's time to eat anyway. I think you ought to go ahead. I wouldn't mind."

Suddenly the dam broke. Polly began planning just how she would manage. I got a picture of how she must have been before she was married, full of vivacity and bounce. By the end of the session, she was proposing that they stay downtown one night a week to go to the theater after she finished the design course she was planning to enroll in.

"And Saturdays," she said, "we can go to the museums together while I catch up on the things I've forgotten. You used to like going with me, didn't you?"

Jerry agreed. And they left the office that day completely involved in plans for the future. It didn't work out that smoothly. By evening, Polly had thought of a million reasons why she couldn't go back to work. And Jerry had become hesitant about the break in their dull routine. They were scared.

But with encouragement and prodding Polly eventually followed through. She was lucky enough to find work almost immediately, part-time work that enabled her to take the courses she felt she needed at the same time. Now she had more than enough to talk about. Jerry was relieved not to have to submit to a cross-examination about his day when he came home every night. In many ways, they seemed like a courting couple—discovering fresh aspects of each other, exclaiming over similarities in likes and dislikes.

Very shortly after this, the couple stopped therapy. All their problems had assumed smaller proportions once they had let a little fun into their lives. Boredom had been eating away at their relationship like a cancer. And with the typical passivity of the Cooperatives, they had done nothing to fight it by themselves.

Part of their problem, of course, was that our society still makes it very difficult for the woman to get married and stay home with her children and then come back into the world. One answer is that the woman keep up with her job after the children are born, but why should she have to? If a woman wants to give her children the best

possible start in life, to enjoy the experience of motherhood, then she should be allowed to do so without being
penalized for it, without having to mortgage the rest of
her life against it.

Another strike against the married woman with children is that when she does decide to reenter the working
world, her age peers are far ahead of her in skills, experience, and position. It is often agonizingly difficult for a
woman who has been queen bee at home to submit to the
discipline of a work situation. Some women, who have
been away from the working world too long, can never
make the adjustment. Fortunately, Polly was not one of
these. She reveled in her new life, and it brought the
sparkle back to the marriage that was needed for its
survival.

Recently I received this letter from Polly, together
with a newspaper clipping of a feature story about her
new job:

Dear Dr. Ravich,
    I certainly hope you remember me—for your influence on me
was very great! Thanks to your advice to "go out and get a job,"
I'm now doing what the enclosed article tells—and loving every
minute of it.
    I started working here six months ago, and I remember only too
well that it was you who gave me the courage to try for something
by telling me that it would only take six months before I'd be back
in the groove. Well, the six months are up—and it surely looks as
if you were right.
    Jerry is simply delighted with my new "career"—and we couldn't
be happier about the whole thing.
    Have a good summer.

                                                Best,
                                                Polly

24

Cooperative:
When Sex Is a Chore

The boredom of the Cooperative pattern extends to sex. Two twenty-five-year-olds fought the battle of the orgasm in my office for a year and a half. They were handsome, healthy, had good jobs—and a terrible sex life. Their four-year-old marriage was very shaky, and they blamed it all on sex.

Sandy said she rarely experienced orgasm. And when she did, it was short, insignificant—and not worth the effort. Harvey claimed that Sandy was unresponsive.

"She just lies there," he said.

"You don't make me feel like anything else," she countered.

Their Train Game graph was a carefully alternating Cooperative pattern, so typical that it was strange to hear them fighting out the battle of the orgasm, since Cooperatives are so fight-phobic. But even this conflict was an act of cooperation, of collusion. They were cooperating in killing their sex life.

If Sandy felt like sex, Harvey didn't. If one was willing to give, the other held back. They were perpetually taking turns in withholding sex and criticizing the other for withholding it. They were playing a symmetrical game that neither one could win.

This type of sexual problem is characteristic of Cooperatives, although the cessation of sexual encounters does not usually become established so early on. They reported that their sex life had been highly satisfactory the first year or so of their marriage, but then it just "went bad."

"It got boring," Harvey said. And Sandy nodded her agreement. "It just wasn't worth the effort," she said.

They had done nothing to make it more interesting. In a typical Cooperative manner, they had not experimented with different positions, different times of day, different places. They had indulged in none of the usual fun or fantasy that many couples enliven their lovemaking with. And they were rather shocked when I discussed this with them.

"This is an area where you need to be generous to each other," I told Sandy and Harvey at the beginning of one session. At this, they both fell silent. That statement froze them. For five minutes, they just sat there, not talking or looking at each other. It was as if I were asking them to do the unthinkable.

And in a way, I was. I was asking them to change one of the basic rules of their marital structure. Their main area of cooperation had been to agree that they would not have satisfactory sex. This had become like a law of the universe. They were not aware of this on a conscious level, but it was as deeply ingrained in their relationship as their habit of brushing their teeth every morning. Now I was asking them to break this law. I was asking them to cooperate in getting closer, instead of cooperating in establishing distance between them.

When Cooperatives have stopped having sex—and this is very common with them—it is like reversing the stars in their courses to get them to resume again. Like Sandy and Harvey, they insist that they want to save their marriage, but they find it impossible to have sex with each other. They sleep in the same bed, live in circumstances of utmost intimacy, dress and undress in front of each other, watch erotic films together—and are never turned on to each other. When they reach this point, it is common for one or both partners to have extramarital affairs in which they may demonstrate great inventiveness in lovemaking and relish every moment of it, but when they come home, they are as shy and awkward with their partners as the most inhibited virgins.

One approach I use with these pairs is to instruct them to make sex dates with each other. We discuss the matter during therapy sessions, and the husband and wife hammer out an agreement that I tell them they must abide by. Sandy and Harvey had the usual reactions of Cooperatives when I proposed this.

"Make a sex date!" Sandy explained. "I couldn't. Sex has to be spontaneous."

"Yeah," Harvey said. "I don't know about you, Doctor, but I can't get it up on command."

I explained to them that what I meant by a sex date was that they were to set aside a certain block of time, from eight in the evening until ten, for instance, in which they would have sex. There were to be no distractions, no television, no excuses. For couples with children, I sometimes suggest that they go to a hotel for the first few dates. This not only gives them privacy, but the fact of paying for the hotel room often makes them feel they have to get their money's worth.

The next step was to have them agree on how often

they wanted to have sex. From the expression on their faces, one would think that once every five years would have been too often, but Harvey finally said that he'd like it three times a week. Sandy bargained him down to twice a week. I suggested they agree on that, since it was twice a week more than they were having sex at the moment.

They walked into my office rather sheepishly at the next session. I waited for them to speak. They sat there. I waited. They became fidgety. Finally Harvey exploded, "Well, it didn't work. I knew it wouldn't. I felt like a damned fool."

"What happened?"

"Nothing."

As they started talking, a ludicrous picture emerged. Ludicrous, but sad. They had finished their dinner at 7:30 on the night they had agreed to have their first sex date, stalled around in the living room reading the paper and watching television until 8:30, the appointed time. Then, without a word, as if they were going to take their medicine, they got up, went into the bedroom, and started undressing. They lay naked on the bed. Finally, they started a conversation about how ridiculous it was of the doctor to expect them to make love in such a planned, unspontaneous manner. They discussed this for two hours, the allotted time, got up, put on their dressing gowns and watched television until they were sleepy.

"A beautiful demonstration of cooperation," I said. "I thought you two were going to practice being generous toward each other."

They began arguing that the lack of spontaneity made it impossible. Every couple uses that argument in these circumstances. And I pointed out that when a man or a woman indulges in an extramarital love affair, there is a minimum of spontaneity involved. Plans have to be made. The time and place usually have to be negotiated carefully. Then when the couple meet, they have one end in mind—lovemaking. There is little spontaneity here. But the meetings are usually delightful, satisfying enough so that both partners look forward to the next encounter and start planning the time and place again.

Sandy and Harvey agreed to keep trying. It was several weeks before they reported they had had a "pleasant" evening. But this was the turning point. Once they proved they could do it, they kept to the schedule— another instance of the Cooperative's restricted imagination. Sandy and Harvey felt that since they were succeeding in the task I had set them, they should continue on at the appointed times.

They stopped therapy shortly after they reported achieving success. Sometimes I wonder whether they are dutifully making love every Tuesday and Saturday night between 8:30 and 10:30.

25

Competitive:
The "Killer" Relationship

The nuclear pair that tests out to the Competitive pattern is usually engaged in a bitter struggle for supremacy. No holds are barred. Tricks and stratagems are marshaled; brute strength and staying power count.

And yet, this can be a delightful mode of interaction if the couple can control the competition instead of letting it drain them. There is spark here and vitality, a richer variety of interaction than in the Dominant-Submissive and Cooperative patterns.

As with the Cooperative, the Competitive pattern is symmetrical; both partners are doing the same thing—competing. Yet, the graph is wild. It shows no tidy zigzags as does the Cooperative graph. Wild swings, collisions, barrier closings mark the Competitive graph. Some players have as many as thirty collisions in the course of one trip. There is no holding back among the Competitives. They try with all the energy and guile at their command to win. And if their opponent is an equal match, the ultimate form of the pure Competitive pattern is what game theory describes as the Minimax Solution, a kind of long-term trench warfare.

The diagram on pp. 164–5 is a typical Competitive graph. The first two-thirds exhibits the characteristic wild swings of the slam-bang competition, while the rigid parallels of the last third represent the entrenched positions of the Minimax Solution.

The Minimax Solution was elegantly illustrated by a group of international trade representatives from African, Latin American, and Oriental nations who met at the World Trade Institute in New York to work out ways for increasing trade among their countries. Their discussions had been lengthy—and unproductive. It was suggested that the Train Game might prove a valuable aid in analyzing their negotiations. The suggestion was accepted.

Without exception, each pair of delegates played the Minimax Solution. One of them called it a "Suez Canal" game, referring to the fact that when the Suez Canal was blocked, *all* ships and tankers had to round the Cape of Good Hope to get from Europe to the Indian Ocean. The competition between these men was intense. None of them dared to lose. More important, none of them dared let his opponent win. The players settled into the mode of play that was most self-protective. Each took the Alternate Route, closing the barrier to prevent his opponent from taking the Direct Route. Both lost—but neither won.

People play this way when they feel that the other is not going to give them a chance. It's a form of all-out war: each wants to save himself by minimizing his losses and not allowing himself to be trapped. But it is not productive. It can drag on until exhaustion or death puts an end to it.

It was easy to understand why the trade conference had been unsatisfactory. The only way this pattern can

| | X = Player A ———— | | |
| | O = Player B —·—··—··— | | |

Barrier	Route & Order of Finish	Direction	INITIAL ... LEARNING
1	1	0	
2	1	0	
1	1	1	
2	1	1	
1	1	2	
2	1	2	
0	1	2	
0	1	0	
0	1	1	
1	0	0	
2	0	0	
1	0	1	
2	0	1	
1	0	2	
2	0	2	
0	0	2	
0	2	0	
0	2	1	
1	2	0	
2	2	0	
1	2	1	
2	2	1	
1	2	2	
2	2	2	
0	2	2	
0	0	0	
0	0	1	
Collision(s)			* * * *
Trip			1 2 3 4 5 6 7

This couple played a typically Competitive game, settling at the end into a no-win/no-loss pattern. (For information on how to interpret this diagram, please refer to p. 61.)

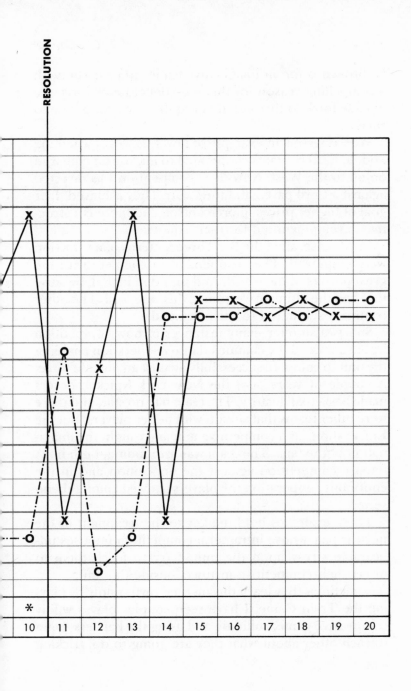

be broken is for an imaginative leader to come up with a compelling reason for them to cooperate or for some outside force to threaten them so that they cooperate to survive.

We witnessed an example of how this works when the Middle Eastern states cooperated to impose an embargo on oil to the West. Now their competition was directed against a third party, and they won. They achieved their goal of higher prices, more control, and more constructive development aid for their countries.

In this case, all of the Big Three patterns of interaction were employed. They cooperated to compete with the great powers of the world. And they dominated, because they had the ultimate weapon in this case—oil. The other countries submitted to their demands.

Sports also offer many instances of how competition within a unit can be channeled into cooperation enabling the unit to compete successfully against an outside force. A couple of years ago, the New York Knickerbockers made basketball history. The team had no star, and there were other teams that season with better players, but the Knicks shone as a competitive unit and caught the imagination of the fans. The team was astounding, both in its intense competition against the opposition and in the enormous cooperation the players showed among themselves.

These examples hold the key to the treatment of the nuclear pair whose intramural competition imposes unbearable stress upon the unit. I try to teach them to direct their competitive instincts ouside the unit.

Sometimes they learn this on their own simply by playing the Train Game. I have seen couples play a wildly competitive game, colliding and using the barriers, lying to each other about what they are going to do, tricking the other—and then, suddenly, deciding to cooperate and beat the game. They work hard at shaving the time down as much as possible. Split seconds become immensely important. This is an exhilarating kind of game, until they have perfected it, but then they can't keep it up. They get bored. The sad fact seems to be that even the most intense form of cooperation gets boring. But as a trade-off from Competitive interaction, it can offer a blessed respite.

More often, their first step in this direction is aimed against the doctor. This is so common that when a couple achieves this, I think of it as their having mastered the "dump the doctor" technique. When the couple is then given to understand that they have succeeded in working together against a third person, they are encouraged to apply their new skill to working together against more rewarding opponents and thus enjoy more of the benefits of cooperation.

One illustration of a successful "dump the doctor" effort was an intensely competitive couple who were also heavy smokers. At one point, I said, "Look, you two, if you give up smoking, I'll give you a free session." They agreed. And from that moment on, they never smoked again in my office. They assured me that they had kicked the habit. But about three months later, I ran into them on the street. Both were smoking. They were embarrassed, but laughed and confessed that they had started smoking two weeks after they had given it up, but had agreed to keep up the fiction in front of me.

I congratulated them. "That's the first example of cooperation I've seen between you. And you carried it off beautifully. You worked together to pull the wool over my eyes."

It really was an achievement. The normal thing for this

couple would have been for one of them to start smoking and the other to tell me about it in an effort to put the partner down.

Competitives are usually easy to treat. They don't tend to run away from therapy like the Dominant-Submissives, nor do they try to turn therapy into a way of life like the Cooperatives. They fight it out between themselves and with the therapist. Always, my aim is to leave them their competitive energy, but get them to direct most of it outside the nuclear unit. This takes a lot of the wear and tear out of the interaction.

Another aim in therapy is to make them more perceptive about each other's feelings and needs. Competitives may not know each other very well, even if they have been married for years and years. They don't tell each other much (and often they lie)—probably out of self-defense, because Competitives enjoy tormenting each other, and will seize on any admission of weakness. Therapy is directed toward helping them become more sympathetic with their partner, learning more about the person they are living with.

Unlike Dominant-Submissives, who use sex to control, and Cooperatives, who turn sex into a ho-hum affair, Competitives usually have a good sex life—even when everything else seems to be cracking up. If the marriage does break up, it is rarely because sex is not good.

Despite the exhaustion that exaggerated, endless competition may bring, the Competitives may have the best marriages of the Big Three patterns of interaction. I am inclined to believe this is so because the Competitive pattern, which occurs in about 11 percent of marriages, draws from both the other patterns. It is usually not difficult for Competitives to switch over to the Cooperative pattern as a nuclear pair, while still retaining their intimate Competitive interaction. And in almost every couple there's a trace of the primitive interaction, Dominant-Submissive. The richer interactive background, which is reflected in the wider competitive range of play in the Train Game, may give them the flexibility and variety needed to overcome the inevitable stresses of all marriages and the particular stresses of competition. The Competitive interaction also forces each member of the pair to attain his full potential. He needs it to survive.

26

Competitive:
The Scrappy Mouse

He was a young business executive. Aggressive, competitive, success oriented. She was his very attractive wife. There were two small children. Claire was an excellent mother, Jack said, but a disappointing wife. Not the wife, he thought, for a rising young man. In our pregame interview he spent a lot of time criticizing the way Claire dressed, the way she responded to the business contacts he brought home, the way she made love—and the way she responded to his ideas.

She was inadequate, he complained. Not the wife he needed. "I need someone who challenges me," he said. "Someone to bring out all the potential in me. Someone who can share my success."

Claire was sitting there weeping silently while her husband outlined her inadequacies and explained his needs. She said very little. He concluded his indictment by saying, "She's really nothing."

On the surface evidence I was inclined to agree with him. She was certainly attractive, but the mousy way she sat there and let him tear her apart, criticize each and

every one of her functions as a woman, seemed to rein-
force his complaints. There was no active response on
her part, no anger, no sullenness, no argument—just
that silent weeping. Maybe she was really nothing. Perhaps that pretty face was just the outside of a vacuum. On
the other hand, tears are a powerful weapon, possibly
more powerful than anger or argument.

Then they played the game. When the graph was fed
back to me by the computer, I was flabbergasted, really
amazed. I had thought she was just a doormat. In my
mind, I had analyzed them as Dominant-Submissives. He
was probably going to mop up the floor with her for the
rest of their marriage—the Dominant-Submissive relationship being so resistant to change.

Well, no such thing. She was as scrappy and competitive as they come. If Jack was looking for a challenger and
a competitor, Claire was it. He just hadn't realized it.
And neither had she. Claire played a cat-and-mouse
game with her husband. She trapped him time after time.
She would play along in a very meek manner, acting
subservient, but Jack could never figure out where her
train was. When he asked, she gave him a misleading
answer. She would tell him she was going to take the
Alternate Route, so Jack would confidently take the Direct Route. Then—zap! She would pounce, close the
barrier, and he was trapped. She had been on the Direct
Route all the time and she had lured him along far
enough so that he could not reciprocate by closing the
barrier on her. A crafty and effective fighter. Certainly a
worthy competitor for her husband.

When I pointed out the significance of their play in the
postgame session, each seemed unbelieving. But then,
bits of evidence came out. As they recounted certain

marital controversies, they both became convinced that Claire was indeed a scrapper who gave Jack as good a run for his money as he gave her. In fact, probably better.

Claire was determined to have a house. Jack wanted to stay on in their apartment. It was convenient and was less expensive than a house would be. He preferred to spend their discretionary money on other things than housing. But Claire's mind was set on a house, and Claire was the one who handled the family budget. Each month, despite Jack's protests, she set aside a sum, so large that it cut down considerably on their standard of living, toward the eventual down payment on a house. And Jack was stymied. Claire held those purse strings.

The game itself provided most of their treatment. They were convinced that there was no way for both of them to come out ahead. Now I reminded them that the instructions had made it clear that both could win. I sat down with them in the testing room and led them through several trips so they could go back over their pattern four or five times. Eventually they realized that it was indeed possible for them to work together, not against each other, and beat the game. That was all it needed.

After about four sessions of therapy, Jack and Claire had more or less straightened themselves out. Each saw himself and his partner through different eyes. Claire became more openly the challenging, aggressive partner that Jack sought. And Jack began to encourage her instead of always putting her down. Just this extra dimension of interaction changed their lives. They became a team who competed against others instead of against each other.

Could this disguised competitive interaction have been predicted in the early days of their marriage? Or before marriage? Yes, if the Train Game had been available. Without this diagnostic tool, it would have taken months and months of therapy to uncover the true interaction within this nuclear pair. It is significant that even as experienced as I am with the typical manifestations of the eight interactive patterns after treating so many couples, my first superficial judgment was way off base. This case corroborated my view that the pattern of interaction is not a superficial manifestation of a relationship, but rather its very structure. It is what goes on within the human atom.

What if Jack and Claire had played the game early in their relationship? What could they have been told if the Competitive pattern had been clear?

First of all, if they had had counseling before marriage, they could have been told just what a slugfest they were going to be involved in. A therapist might have been able to explain to them that they should work on channeling their competition against outside forces rather than each other as much as possible.

Then, in this particular case, many of their problems arose because their outer behavior did not correspond to their inner, true behavior. They were fighting in the dark because of Claire's deceptively meek and mousy manner. This deceptive exterior was probably imposed by our culture, at least to some extent. She was acting the way she thought she should act as a woman and a wife, and not the way she felt. If both of them could have been helped to get in touch with their own true feelings before marriage, they could have stopped this fighting in the dark. It could have been brought out into the open. The

task here, as in all such cases, is for the therapist to make
people aware of the situation so that they do not fool
themselves about what they are doing and what is going
on between them.

27

Competitive: Two Generations of Gate Flickers

Claire, the scrappy mouse of the last chapter, used to lure her husband onto the Direct Route by leaving the barrier open, then closing it at the very last moment, forcing him to reverse and take the Alternate Route—or sit immobilized until she finished. Either way, he lost.

This was a mild or moderate use of what I call Gate Flicking—using the barrier as a come-on device. But some Competitives make the Scrappy Mouse look like the gentlest puller of punches. They play that barrier as if it were a violin, now luring the opponent on, trapping him, forcing him to retreat, luring again, raising hopes, slamming the barrier down—only to relent (or so it seems) when the opponent has accepted defeat and started to reverse, deceiving him into advancing again—and once again trapping him.

This takes great verve, energy, and perception. Especially perception, since the Gate Flickers cannot see over the dividing panel and have to guess where their partner's train is. They ask questions, but get either no answers, misleading answers, or downright untruthful answers. Their play is dramatic, full of hairbreadth decisions. Will the opponent squeak past the barrier because his opposite has misjudged position or timing? And what is the opponent planning to do? Is he going to wield the barrier as his ultimate weapon, too? There is a tremendous battle for supremacy here. Who will win the battle of the barrier?

I recall one couple in treatment who were incurable Gate Flickers. I could not get them to understand that this was the least productive of all forms of play for them as a couple, that it not only was unproductive, but fanned the competitive flames of their relationship. They would agree, insist that they understood what I was talking about—and immediately proceed to demonstrate that they did not.

In their mutual, everyday life, they fought about everything. They disputed who was more tired at the end of the day. They squabbled over who would get the outside slice of a roast of beef—even though a roast has two outside slices. They argued over which route to take to the beach, over their budget, the children, the dog. One famous battle involved the game of Monopoly. They got so absorbed in it that they played for sixteen hours straight, each trying to wipe the other out.

Their competition was truly enervating. Greta and Jerry were emotionally—and to a degree physically—exhausted when they first came to me. Jerry was the head of a small company with a seasonal business. During the peak seasons, he had to put in long hours. Over the years, Greta, in a kind of revenge for Jerry's absorption in his work, had consoled herself for his absence by having a series of affairs. None of them were particularly serious, but Jerry had found out about the last one. And he was almost murderously jealous. She retaliated by accusing him of seeing other women, something that she did not really believe; it was just a handy verbal weapon. But Jerry, thinking that Greta had found him out, admitted that he had been having an affair for several years. It was his ultimate secret weapon against Greta. Now the fat was in the fire. There was a battle royal that lasted for weeks. Jerry moved out of the house, then back in. Greta left him, then returned. Finally, their family doctor, to whom Jerry had gone asking for tranquilizers, referred them to me.

Like many Competitives, they responded well to treatment. Their love affairs had been relatively meaningless. In fact, Jerry seemed relieved to have an excuse to terminate his. And Greta had always changed lovers with the seasons, almost the way she changed her wardrobe. Dropping these outside "interests" was the first step toward easing their relationship—and the easiest one. While it did lessen the tension, it was difficult to get the two of them focused on an outside object, a third party against whom they could compete.

The stumbling block was that, although their infighting exhausted them, each delighted in it, relished every time he or she was one-up on the other. It was life itself to them. At the same time, both Greta and Jerry acknowledged that it was no way to live.

One natural outlet for their competition was sports. I encouraged them to get involved in games in which they teamed up against other couples or against the game itself. A physical outlet is useful since it both channels the competitive urge and yields physical and emotional relaxation—fatigue without stress. They both liked table tennis, so they decided to play in an organized way and join tournaments at their club. But this only intensified the competition, since they were really playing against each other to see who would get highest on the tournament ladder. Their next choice was paddle tennis, which had the advantage of being an outdoor sport they could play together in winter, as well as one in which the sexes were fairly equal players—and they could play doubles. They also were murder at a bridge table, but now understood that they had to play as a couple. This helped a lot.

But politics proved to be the most constructive outlet for their competition and one they had never tried before. Greta got involved first, when I suggested she find something to do with the time on her hands during those seasons when Jerry had to work late. She became absolutely fascinated with the mechanics of a local campaign, got Jerry interested, and soon they were working as a team to put over their candidate. Now, all their excess energies go into politics. It is a continuing and meaningful effort for them. They feel that they are accomplishing something—together.

The combination of all these outside activities diminished the emotional overload on the marital system. Not that they stopped fighting—that would be an unrealistic expectation. They are always in a state of excitement about something or other—but they like it. Perfect harmony would drive them crazy. What they needed was to tilt the seesaw a little, so that life was not all competition. Introducing an element of cooperation restored a livable balance to their lives.

They were just about ready to terminate therapy when they came in one day in great distress. "Wendy is pregnant," Greta announced. Wendy, their seventeen-year-old daughter, was a pretty girl. She had been going around with a young man, one year older, for more than a year. The families had accepted that Wendy and Sherwin would probably get married when they finished college.

"She's six weeks pregnant," Greta said.

"What is she going to do?" I asked, knowing that, since they were Catholics, the answer probably would not be abortion.

"We've discussed it," Jerry said. "We've decided that she should have the baby. She can go stay with Greta's sister in Toronto until it comes, and then we will put it up for adoption."

I was disturbed by the consistent use of "we" as Greta and Jerry explained how they were going to handle the problem. This couple was cooperating very smoothly now and working together to solve this problem, but what about the people most intimately concerned— Wendy and her boyfriend, the father of this unborn child? And, yes, that unborn baby, too.

"Why don't you ask Wendy and Sherwin to come see me?" I suggested. "This is a very heavy problem for two young people to handle."

The parents agreed, and a few days later Wendy and Sherwin came in to talk and to play the Train Game.

Sherwin was beyond any doubt very much in love with Wendy. As they talked, it became clear that they intended to continue their relationship and were looking forward to the day when they would be independent and could get married. This was no casual boy-girl affair. They had been going around for a year and a half, and even this unwanted pregnancy had not shaken them.

"What about getting married?" I asked. "Getting married now, before the baby arrives?"

Sherwin looked at me. "How can we?" he asked. "I have a part-time job to earn money for college. Wendy's still in high school. She should go on to college. It would ruin her life."

Wendy's father spoke up. "They're too young to get married," Jerry said. "Maybe later. But not now. They're too young."

"How old were you when you and Greta got married?" I asked, knowing the answer.

"I was seventeen," Greta said. "And so was Jerry."

"Well?"

"But we were more responsible," Jerry said.

"Sherwin's parents agree with us," Greta added. "They think the children should wait a few years before getting married."

Sherwin and Wendy now went into the testing room to play the Train Game. The session was over.

I was very concerned. The idea of Wendy, a bright, sensitive girl, bearing a child who would be put up for adoption, a child whom she would never see again, seemed to me unnecessarily brutal. And what a shadow to cast over the rest of the lives of these two young people! What a terrible burden to carry through life, to know that you had a child and not know where the child was, whether or not it was thriving and happy, what kind of life it had. No matter that Wendy would probably have other children, her firstborn would always be lost to her —and to Sherwin. And the burden would not be confined to them; it would rest on the grandparent generation as well. This child would be the first grandchild on either side of the family.

As the computer printed out the graph of Wendy's and Sherwin's interaction as they played the Train Game, I was struck by the pattern that evolved. Wendy and Sherwin played a Competitive game. Not only that, their pattern was very similar to that of Greta and Jerry. Wendy played just the way her mother did; Sherwin's play very much resembled that of her father. Their employment of Gate Flicking as a competitive weapon was equally as shrewd as that of the older generation, although their play was not quite so cutthroat.

I considered. Greta and Jerry now had a happy enough marriage. They had mastered the ability to direct their competition outside instead of within the nuclear pair.

I talked to Jerry and Greta, showed them the young couple's graph, and explained what a heavy psychological burden they were placing on their daughter—a lifetime burden.

"This is too severe a punishment to inflict," I said. "Its enormity is not so apparent now, but when Wendy has her second child—well, I wonder if she will be able to enjoy it and love it in the wholehearted way she should. She will always have guilt about her firstborn.

"These two are in love," I said. "It's a steady kind of relationship. Their interaction almost duplicates your own interaction. And you've had a good marriage on the whole, haven't you?"

They agreed. They had never stopped loving each other, even when things were at their worst.

"Both you and Sherwin's parents are talking in terms of them getting married 'later,' " I said. "Why not now? Why not let them keep their baby? I think they're ready. Can't you work something out? The six of you?"

Jerry and Greta were ready to be convinced. So were Sherwin's parents. The young couple was beamingly happy. I talked to them about the significance of their pattern, explained how strenuous, unrelenting competition can sap the psychic energy that should go into more rewarding channels.

Sherwin said, "You're really telling us that when we get into a fight, we should ask ourselves, What are we fighting about and who can we fight instead?"

"Something like that," I said. "When you are aware that you're fighting, that's half the battle. That's the signal to refocus your competition. But you also have to learn to recognize the disguised forms of competition and handle those before they get too stressful."

Wendy nodded. "Like Mom and Dad," she agreed. "I remember when they even used to fight about who had more difficulty sleeping. My mother would say, 'I didn't sleep a wink all night.' And my father would reply, 'Well you certainly were sleeping like a baby when I finally came back to bed at five o'clock. I was up all night reading.' Mom would be furious."

I nodded. "Now about the matter of my fee," I joked. They immediately became very serious. "I want you to promise to bring that baby in to play the Train Game when he or she decides to get married."

They agreed that it was a reasonable enough "fee."

28

Competitive: The Minimax Solution

In some nuclear pairs, the Competitive interaction develops into a kind of trench warfare, so fierce, so deadly that neither dares give the other an inch. The partners work out a way to play the Train Game in which both lose, but neither can possibly win—and the latter is the more important consideration. I gave an example of this type of competition in the world of international trade (page 163), but the homegrown variety, the Minimax Solution enacted by a husband and wife, can be infinitely more vicious.

Vanessa and Frederick Archer were vicious fighters who had lived in a state of siege for years, even though they operated a successful business together, a business in which each partner's talents were fully utilized and which paid off financially. Vanessa had a definitive knowledge of antiques, design, and fabrics, an unerring eye for good line. Frederick was a shrewd businessman with a flair for promotion. Together they had built up a chain of boutiques in resort towns—New England in the summer, Florida in the winter. Vanessa did the buying;

Frederick took care of all the business end of things, including promotion and advertising.

As they explained this in the pregame session, it seemed to be a perfect example of a Cooperative relationship where each was able to fulfill his potential in working toward the common goal. But no such thing. It was jarring even to be in the room with them. They had come to me because they had reached an impasse. It was a matter of how to spend their vacation. Frederick wanted to go off alone with three other men on a canoe trip through the Canadian wilderness. Vanessa insisted that he go with her to Europe. She could not understand his wanting to go on vacation without her. Frederick had suggested a compromise, that they take a second vacation later on—together. And he would go wherever Vanessa suggested. In the meantime, she could go to Europe alone. She had friends there. And he was adamant about his own plans. The canoe trip was something he would not give up. Vanessa would not agree. The battle raged. Each had retreated to dug-in positions. Finally they had come to me.

Their Train Game graph settled very quickly into the Competitive Minimax Solution pattern. There was not an iota of cooperation evinced in their play. After a few wild, swinging, challenging trips, they both settled down into the Minimax Solution. Both started out each trip by clenching their teeth, closing their barriers, and sending their trains off on the Alternate Route, time after time after time. They played grimly, as if each were facing execution. And neither wavered from the Minimax pattern once it had been established that this was the only sure way to prevent the other player from finishing first.

They conducted their marriage along Minimax lines as

well. Each accepted a minimum loss in order to avoid the other's gaining any slight advantage. Everything was a fight, and none of the fights was ever resolved. They had been fighting for six years about whether or not to have children. Frederick would say, "I don't want a child as long as our relationship is like this." And Vanessa would retort, "Well, if I cannot be sure that our marriage will last, I think you should give me half the shops for my own, so that I'll have something to fall back on." Then the fight would jump over into the divorce arena. Should they get a divorce? Did they want a divorce? What would the grounds be? And how should they split up the business?

Competition pervaded every aspect of their lives. One upstairs room had never been furnished because they could not agree on its use. Vanessa thought it should be a charming sitting room/study. Frederick thought it should be kept for a child's room in case they decided to have a baby. And then back they would be into the dispute over whether or not to have a child.

The first step in therapy was to enforce a little peace in the relationship, a temporary reprieve from fighting, to provide a little space where each could relax. The constant fighting had worn them to a frazzle.

I suggested that Frederick go ahead with his vacation plans and that Vanessa also take a vacation or stay home or do whatever she wanted, but that Frederick's trip be confined to one week so that they would be able to take a long vacation together later on.

Vanessa grudgingly agreed, but only, as she made clear, because she wanted to show me, the therapist, that she was not resisting treatment.

She decided to stay home while Frederick went off to

Canada with his pals. When they showed up in my office again, ten days later, they were on demonstrably better terms. Frederick had not enjoyed his vacation. And had said so. The weather had been terrible, cold and wet. His friends had not worn well under the unaccustomed hardship of outdoor living. He was glad to be home. Vanessa was so jubilant over her "victory," which consisted of having Frederick admit he had a rotten time, that she was all sunshine and cheer.

This didn't last long. They returned to the usual infighting. They simply could not transfer their very effective cooperative relationship in business to their personal lives. Everything turned into a fight. At one session, we started listing some of the subjects that had provoked open fights during the past week. They started laughing as the list grew to ten, then twenty items and both were still contributing more fight-provoking incidents or statements. It seemed that there was not a subject or circumstance in their mutual life that they did not fight over.

Eventually, one of their fights escalated to the point where Vanessa walked out of the house. She not only walked out, but rented a small apartment and refused to come home. But she went to work. Every morning she showed up and carried on her routine of inspecting merchandise and buying for their boutiques. And Frederick did the same. He carried on his responsibilities just exactly as before.

At this point, I started seeing them each separately instead of together. I wanted to know how each one was getting along, what was in their heads, how distressed they really were—and whether they were finding any satisfaction in their lives apart. It would have been impossible for Vanessa and Frederick to discuss their feelings openly in front of the other at this point.

I was not particularly surprised to learn that each was managing quite well. There was hurt and bitterness, but no particular misery or heartbreak. Both were so grateful for the respite from fighting that this took precedence over all their other feelings.

They never did get back together again—as husband and wife, that is. The separation became formalized. The family assets were divided; legal steps were taken to give each a half-interest in the business; and they continued their business relationship amicably and successfully.

Some Competitive pairs are so fatigued by a marital lifetime of constant fighting that they do not have the energy or desire to make the necessary interactional shift to redirect their aggressions outside the marriage. Jerry and Greta, the Gate Flickers (see page 176) had managed to do it, but the Archers' competition had been too bitter, too intense. The nuclear pair was burned out. There was nothing left. If the fire of competition burns too fiercely, the human atom becomes like a cold star where nothing happens.

In these cases, there is little a therapist can do except preside over the breakup, treat the emotional wounds, and try to help both halves of the fissioned pair learn how to function apart. Since very few divorces ever mark a complete end of the relationship, the competition (and the mutual interest, even fascination) often continues—but in a more manageable, less damaging form because there is more physical and emotional space between the pair.

In the case of Vanessa and Frederick Archer, their

business relationship was solidly based and had a definite Cooperative cast. They were intent on making their shops successful, and they succeeded. This area of interaction had always been a pleasure to them and it continued to be one even after their formal separation.

In some cases where the Competitive pair divorces, the competition is still so great that the former mates compete to remarry a richer, more important, more attractive, more whatever person. They like to lord it over their previous spouses. They also tend to reopen custody decisions and fight over the children. Often they try to make allies of the children, woo them with gifts and indulgences.

When these pairs divorce, then, the therapist plays an important role. He has to work with each individual to help him understand that there is no profit in competing against his former mate, that this kind of fighting only weakens his abilities to form a new and more satisfying relationship.

29

The Minor Four

The Minor Four are the combinations of the Big Three interactions: Dominant-Submissive/Competitive; Dominant-Submissive/Cooperative; Cooperative/Competitive; and Dominant-Submissive/Cooperative/Competitive. The most striking aspect of all four is the dissatisfaction and unhappiness of the nuclear pair exhibiting these mixed interactions. One might expect that the ability to interact in more than one major way would not only relieve much of the stress of a pair relationship but also enrich it. I was almost convinced that I would find this to be true when I started classifying and observing the interactive patterns, because in treating couples who exhibited a more or less "pure" version of one of the Big Three patterns, the introduction of an alternate mode of interaction proved to be the most effective therapy. I suspected that I would find that the couples who had an innate, natural mastery of two or more modes of interaction would be able to cope masterfully with the stresses of dyadic life.

This did not prove to be so. Indeed, those couples testing out to a hybrid pattern were among the unhappiest of my patients. Their lives were unstable, explosive.

It was as if they were living in the middle of a mine field.

I have come to believe that this happens because in the majority of cases the hybrid interactions involve a continual shift back and forth between complementary and symmetrical interactions. The pure Dominant-Submissive pattern, for instance, is a complementary relationship. Someone is always leading, someone is always following. The Cooperative and Competitive patterns, on the other hand, are symmetrical. Each partner does the same thing—cooperates or competes.

In the Minor Four, three of the interactive patterns require a shift between complementary and symmetrical. Two of these patterns, Dominant-Submissive/Competitive and Dominant-Submissive/Cooperative, account for 28 percent of all married couples.[22]

An examination of the Dominant-Submissive/Competitive and the Dominant-Submissive/Cooperative, the two interactive patterns balanced more or less evenly between complementary and symmetrical interactions, reveals the friction that can be generated by dynamic, 180-degree shifts.

30

Dominant-Submissive/ Competitive: Nuclear Explosives

If there is one way in which Dominant-Submissive/Competitive is a "healthier" pattern of interaction than the Dominant-Submissive, it may be the ability of these pairs to split the human atom when the relationship gets unbearably abrasive; at least they find it easier than the pure Dominant-Submissive nuclear pair. This hybrid group represents about 16 percent of couples seeking marital therapy and is the third largest category, ranking after Dominant-Submissive (26 percent) and Cooperative (20 percent).

There is a tremendous amount of tension in these relationships, as one might expect, knowing what we do about the Dominant-Submissives and about the Competitives. The strife and fatigue of the Competitive are coincident here with the stress and exaggerated interdependency of the Dominant-Submissive. The cases that come to me can be characterized as noisy, stress-wracked, full of misery. Both partners hurt. So there is no cynicism implied when I say that the positive element in this pattern is that couples can be separated if tensions cannot be lessened. Also, they have a capacity for change.[23] They are not self-condemned, as are the Dominant-Submissives, to live unhappily ever after.

One of the most intricate and interesting cases I have treated in this category is that of Frank and Sonia Walton. Or, more correctly, the cases of the Waltons and of Frank Walton and Alice Evans.

The Waltons were a battling couple. They had separated, reconciled, separated, reconciled so many times that neither could remember how many. When they came to me, Frank was living with Alice, his girlfriend. Frank's affair with Alice had gone on for about three years, a period that had seen the Waltons break up and get back together again several times. Each time, Frank would move in with Alice.

Sonia had decided that she wanted a divorce. But she wanted more than a mere divorce. She was vindictive. She wanted to break up Frank's relationship with Alice. To accomplish this, she was asking for their house, their two cars, 75 percent of Frank's salary for child support and alimony. She was also insisting that the divorce agreement specify that Frank be forbidden to see his children as long as he continued his relationship with Alice.

The lawyers' fees were mounting as the bitterness between Frank and Sonia escalated. This was the competitive aspect of their interaction. Frank had dug in and was refusing to give Sonia anything she asked for as long as she opposed his relationship with his girlfriend.

But now, in a sudden switch, Frank had proposed that they make one more try to save their marriage. He said he wanted to move back home with Sonia and the children. At this point, even the lawyers threw up their hands and suggested that they both get some psychiatric advice. They consulted me, played the Train Game, and their play graphed out (see pp. 194–5) to the Dominant-Submissive/Competitive pattern with its opposing symmetrical-complementary interactions.

When some of my colleagues begin to study interactive patterns, they ask why this hybrid deserves its own category. They suggest that it may simply be a variation of the Dominant-Submissive pattern. After all, they observe, since one person usually wins, this fits the Dominant-Submissive frame. But the computer graph shows the difference in interaction—and very clearly. These are no characteristic parallel lines with the occasional Flip-flop of the Dominant-Submissive. And there is no question of its being a variation of the pure Competitive pattern, since in that pattern, evenly matched partners usually make certain that neither one clearly wins.

Sonia was the Dominant in this pair. This was demonstrated in the way she had marshaled all her weapons to make Frank do what she wanted him to. After a few sessions with the two of them, it was obvious that the marriage was over—even though Frank had moved back home. Sonia was simply fighting for time, fighting to wear Frank out so that he would accede to her demands. There was no way that these two could get back together again.

Frank did not want the marriage to end. He was very dependent on Sonia, but Sonia had made the break intellectually and emotionally, so the mere fact of Frank's physical presence did not mean a thing. And one evening when he came home, she simply shoved a packed suit-

X = Frank Walton ——————
O = Sarah Walton —·—··—··—

Barrier	Route & Order of Finish	Direction							
1	1	0							
2	1	0							
1	1	1							
2	1	1							
1	1	2							
2	1	2							
0	1	2							
0	1	0							
0	1	1							
1	0	0							
2	0	0							
1	0	1							
2	0	1							
0	2	0							
0	2	1							
1	2	0							
2	2	0							
1	2	1							
2	2	1							
1	2	2							
2	2	2							
0	2	2							
0	0	0							
0	0	1							
		Collision(s)					*		
		Trip	1	2	3	4	5	6	7

During the Resolution phase, Frank and Sonia Walton showed a Dominant-Submissive and Competitive pattern of interaction, with collisions occurring on all but the fourteenth, sixteenth, and twentieth trips. (For information on how to interpret this diagram, please refer to p. 61.)

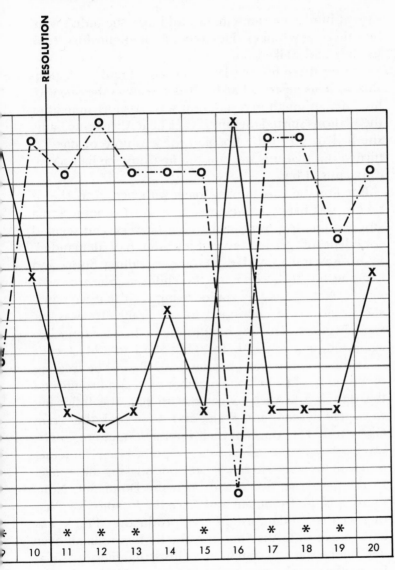

case at him as he came in and told him she didn't want him there any longer. He acceded, made no fuss, took the bag and walked out.

During these few weeks of therapy, Frank's relationship with his mistress had been as stormy as the one with his wife, although in a different way. A short time after the Waltons started therapy, Frank beat Alice up so badly she had to go to the hospital for a couple of days. It turned out that this was not the first time he had physically abused her.

But now he was moving back with her. And she, it seems, was happy to welcome him. At this point Sonia stopped therapy, went back to her lawyers, and seemed confident of getting everything she had demanded. Frank was unhappy. He was always calling Sonia and begging her to let him see the children. She was adamant. "Not as long as you're living with that woman," she would say. I continued to see Frank. He was extremely upset. One day he told me he had beaten Alice again, not as badly as before, but she had a black eye.

At this point, it was obvious that I should be treating that dyad too, not just one member of it, and I suggested that Frank ask Alice to come with him the following week. He agreed, and Frank and Alice took the Train Game test. The graph of their interaction, interestingly, was essentially the same as the graph of Frank's interaction with his wife. There was only one striking difference: In the first case, Sonia had been the Dominant. Now, Frank was the Dominant and Alice the Submissive. Neither of these relationships was productive. Frank was able to live with Alice because she let him walk all over her, but he was still caught up in his struggle with Sonia. In an effort to placate her, he gave in to all her demands, hoping that she would relent and let him see the children. This did not work, and he gave in on that point, too. However, he continued living with Alice. And he continued telephoning his soon-to-be former wife, begging to be allowed to see the children. She always refused.

But this problem almost solved itself. Frank and Alice lived only a short distance from Sonia and the children. It was simplicity itself for Frank to walk over to his old neighborhood and meet the children when they were playing outside. And Sonia seemed to accept this. She made no trouble about his visits with the kids, despite all her previous threats. Eventually, he started taking them to the movies or out for dinner or to a baseball game, all the awkward resorts of the divorced father. And he was able to see them as often as he wished.

The relationship with Alice took somewhat longer to straighten out. The Competitive aspect here was more subtle, although it took a physical form. Alice was often the one who initiated their fights. She would become angry with Frank and slap his face. He would retaliate with more strength. Or Frank would go into a jealous rage and she would taunt him, "Oh, you're just looking for an excuse to hit me. Go ahead. Hit me. You bully." And he would.

During the time I saw Frank, Alice suffered several beatings. There was the one that put her in the hospital. Another time she had a black eye. Once Frank had an ugly scratch down the side of his cheek.

Neither of them wanted to get married. Frank had used Alice as a way of getting "even" with Sonia. When their relationship ended, he had no need for the weapon any longer. Eventually, with one last fight, Alice and Frank broke up too.

Most Dominant-Submissive / Competitive relationships are somewhat less pathological than this one, but the essence of the interaction is caught vividly in these two nuclear pairs, which had one unit (Frank) in common. They are hostile, stormy, upsetting in every aspect. And despite this, there is a closeness, a bond that only serves to intensify the hatred that springs up.

The fact that we do not see more than this 16-percent segment of these couples in therapy suggests that some have been able to handle this difficult blend of complementary and symmetrical interactions in a way that is, if not rewarding (and it may be to some), at least bearable. But I know that if a young couple testing out to this pattern were to come to me for my advice, I would explain to them very carefully what a difficult life might be in store for them. I would back up my gloomy forecast with several examples from my practice, so that they would have situations and individuals to identify with. This, I hope, would give them some knowledge of how the stress implicit in this pattern manifests itself. And I would suggest that if they ever felt their relationship was getting too tense, too stormy, they consult a qualified professional. It could be that therapy at a very early stage could prevent a lot of unhappiness. At least, it could help preserve each partner's emotional and psychological health.

31

Dominant-Submissive/ Cooperative: Quiet Desperation

Here again are two ways of interacting joined together in one relationship within a single structure. One is symmetrical, the other asymmetrical, or complementary; they are absolute opposites. Unlike the actively unhappy Dominant-Submissive/Competitive pattern, this one, although usually disturbed, is calmer. There is friction, but seldom hate. The Dominant-Submissive rigidity is somewhat softened by the Cooperative reasonableness. Treatment usually consists of trying to redistribute the emphasis within the interaction, of shifting the focus away from the Dominant-Submissive sector to the Cooperative sector.

Ethel and Charles Welles not only had an unhappy marriage, but Charles was an alcoholic. Their Train Game trips graphed out to a striking Dominant-Submissive/Cooperative pattern. They went from a Dominant-Submissive opening to Cooperative and back to Dominant-Submissive. During the Cooperative interval, they had collision after collision.

When we discussed their play in the postgame session, I asked, "Why did you have so many collisions in this series of trips?"

"I didn't know that there was a way we could both win at the beginning," Ethel said. "We would collide, and I got tired of waiting for Charles to back down, so I backed down."

This was absolutely no explanation for the staggering number of collisions, but it was an interesting answer, since the graph showed very clearly that Charles was the one who backed down, not Ethel. She had backed away from a collision only twice during the whole game.

The addictive pattern was very clear in their game playing (see Chapter 11, "The Hit-and-Runners"). Ethel said she had not realized Charles was an alcoholic before they were married. She herself had been a heavy drinker (in fact, they had met at a bar) but insisted that she knew when she got married that she could cut down on her drinking. And she said that she had. The big problem was that Ethel felt that since she had cut down, Charles could too. She was also convinced that he wanted to cut down on his drinking, just as she had. Neither of her assumptions was correct: Alcohol was an addiction with Charles.

The same insensitivity had been reflected in the way Ethel played the Train Game. She had said she did not care whether she won or lost. She found the game boring, and so, she was convinced, did Charles. But he didn't. He had not found the game boring. "Frightening" would have been a more accurate description. And he resented bitterly that Ethel was winning all the time. But he was so full of guilt about his drinking and so afraid that she would leave him that he did not dare say anything; he just backed down every time they had a collision.

The significant fact was that it was Charles who initiated the move toward the Cooperative pattern. It was as if he were trying to get in touch with his wife, as if he were trying to say, "Look, let's do things together. I want you to be more interested in doing things with me." And when he collided with her, it was a way of sending a message, "Here I am. Let's stay in touch. Don't go away and leave me." Then he would back away from the collision so Ethel would not be angry with him. And eventually Ethel seemed to get the message and they settled down to an effective, although collision-studded, Cooperative mode of play.

But then Ethel got bored. It was as if she in turn were saying, "That was interesting, but I've had enough of this 'After you, Alphonse' business. I want to have things my way. I want to run this game." And back they went to a Dominant-Submissive pattern, Ethel back to dominating. It came out in therapy that Ethel felt she had to do everything and be responsible for everything because Charles was an alcoholic. And this made her angry. She wanted him to take more responsibility. But when he started to take responsibility, just as when he made the overtures that led to instituting a Cooperative form of play, she could not allow him to continue, because of her own needs. She could not tolerate for very long a relationship in which she was not the boss.

The problem was to get Ethel to accept Charles's efforts toward taking responsibility and to encourage his shows of strength. She had been unconsciously sabotaging all his efforts to stop drinking, while at the same time professing to believe that Charles wanted to stop drink-

ing and that he could stop drinking—if he wanted to—
a dubious bit of tangled-up logic, but it reflected her
confused feelings about his alcoholism. She wanted him
to stop, but she was afraid of the consequences.

I worked with them on trying to shift the cycles of
Dominant-Submissive and Cooperative, to lengthen the
Cooperative cycle and shorten the Dominant-Submissive, but with very little result. The Dominant-Submissive resistance to change was so strong in this pair that
it overpowered the Cooperative part. Not only that, but
it also seemed to strengthen the least desirable aspect of
the Cooperative pattern—the fear that underlies most
Cooperative relationships.

Charles went off on a binge about three months after
they started therapy, and Ethel used this as an excuse to
say that all this soul-searching was getting her husband
too upset. She telephoned me one day and said that she
had decided to stop therapy. Again, a typical Dominant-
Submissive reaction as soon as change threatens.

The pulls of these symmetrical-asymmetrical relationships seem to be as strong as the ocean tides. The pair
goes from one interaction in which there is a kind of
psychic meshing, an interlocking of needs, to another in
which each partner sits at the end of an evenly balanced
emotional seesaw. But when the seesaw tilts, the two
equal partners are suddenly transformed into a solid
force and a weak one; inequality has replaced equality.
One partner becomes heavier and controls the motion of
the seesaw because of his superior strength.

These swift changes are too psyche-shattering for
some couples to cope with. People who belong to this
pattern should know that they need immense reservoirs
of inner strength to be able to survive emotionally. But

it is possible to survive, and that's important. I believe that it would have been possible for Charles and Ethel to have conquered their problems if they had dared do more work on them, instead of clinging like frightened children to the misery that was familiar.[24]

32

Competitive/ Cooperative: When Togetherness Is Too Much

This wedding of two symmetrical, but diametrically opposite, interactions accounts for approximately 5 percent of all nuclear pairs. A contradictory way of interaction—let's compete; let's cooperate—it has a built-in self-destruct mechanism. Some partners can't cooperate and compete simultaneously, so they shift from one to the other, back and forth. Others join the contradictory modes together so that each victory is immediately followed by a defeat.

Both variants are dramatic when seen on a graph. The couples will start playing, for instance, using the barrier frequently, gate flicking to lure the other onto the Direct Route. Or their play will have many slam-bang collisions. Then, suddenly, peace is declared, and they play to beat the game, instead of each other. A few trips later, just as suddenly, they are back to battle positions. The switch is usually instantaneous. Or in the other type, the graph will look somewhat like an alternating pattern, except that the back-and-forth swings will be wider and more irregular.

Fortunately, it's a rare coupling. This pattern includes many loving couples who cannot seem to cope with the humdrum intimacies of marriage, no matter how much they love each other. It is an interaction that in practice is far better suited to friendship than to marriage or any long-term intimate commitment.

In treating a couple who test out to a pure Competitive pattern, I try to introduce an alternate mode of interaction, the Cooperative, and in treating Cooperatives, I have found that helping them learn to interact competitively is often effective therapy; but a couple with a natural mastery of both interactions seems headed for disaster. There is very little stability in these relationships. Love? Yes. And affection, passion, tenderness, understanding, even humor—all these. But even all this is not enough to allow a Cooperative/Competitive to maintain a long-term intimate relationship.

I stress intimate, because these couples have one common characteristic—a space problem. They get along fine as long as they are not forced to live in close proximity. Even a little togetherness may be too much for them.

Stan and Natalie Carpenter were an absolutely typical Competitive/Cooperative couple. They loved each other and had been married for four years when they came to see me, having lived together for three years before getting married. The reasons they gave for their marital problems were silly; they just didn't make sense. And both Stan and Natalie put them forth rather tentatively, as if they knew they were silly reasons—things like different ideas about bedtime, disputes about whether the cleaning woman was doing a good job—all insignificant. They fought a lot, but not excessively and not about any important issues. Most of the time, they said, they had a good time together.

In the pregame session they told me that shortly after they were married they had moved to Chicago, where Stan had been offered a good job. Rents were reasonable, compared to New York, and they were able to afford a comfortable, roomy apartment, larger than they really needed. After a couple of years, Stan decided that the Chicago job offered no chance to get ahead, so they moved back to New York. Here they had to make do with a smaller apartment; it was all they could afford. Most young couples in Manhattan make do with similar apartments very happily. They had a bedroom, a living room, and a kitchen. But they both felt stifled.

Stan said, "We were living in each other's pockets. I couldn't breathe." And for no other reason that he could explain, he moved out.

A few months later, he was offered a job in Houston, Texas. It sounded promising, a chance for a new start. And Natalie agreed to go with him. They had been seeing each other regularly, although Stan had not moved back to the apartment.

In Houston, they were able to rent a house. Stan liked the job. Natalie also found a job. And everything was fine for a while. But they missed New York. After a year, they decided to take a chance that Stan could find something equally promising in New York and they moved back. Again they had to move into a small apartment.

It was the same story all over again. They felt pressured, crowded. And Stan moved out again. At this point, they made a mutual decision to get counseling.

They loved each other, and they wanted to learn how to live together.

They played the Train Game, and their graph was the hybrid Competitive/Cooperative pattern. There was no question that space, or the lack of it, played an important part in their relationship—emotional space as well as physical space. And the two were very closely connected.

My first suggestion was that they make whatever sacrifices were necessary to rent a larger apartment. I pointed out that Manhattan was not the only place to live in New York City, that apartments were less expensive in Brooklyn or Queens. But they were horrified. They had a snobbism that would not allow them to live in one of the "bourgeois boroughs," as Stan put it.

We then explored other ways of providing them with the space cushion they so obviously needed. They eventually decided that if each of them was to take on some outside activity that would keep them occupied two or three evenings a week, it would introduce the element of distance. Natalie immediately enrolled in a crafts course that met evenings, and Stan took on a part-time job. Now they were home together only on weekends and one evening a week.

They reported that life seemed less abrasive with this arrangement. But a few weeks later, Stan's moonlighting job stopped. He found nothing to replace it. In another few weeks, Natalie's course was over, and there was a month's vacation before the next semester began. They were back at where they had started. The temporary distance had disappeared, and it was too much for them to cope with. Stan moved out.

After a few more sessions, they terminated therapy. Stan had rented an apartment. Neither one of them had any outside love interest. And they were on amicable terms with each other. In fact, rather more than amicable.

Six months later they came back to see me. They were thinking of getting back together again. They had found that they were spending most of their spare time with each other, and Stan often spent the night with Natalie. I asked them what was wrong with the present relationship if they were getting along so well. And when it came right down to it, when they stopped taking the societal norm as their norm,[25] they decided that this style of living together apart or living apart together was very acceptable to them.

Most of the cases I see that fall into this pattern do not resolve themselves quite so satisfactorily. But they all have the common elements of true affection between the partners and an absolute inability to tolerate much intimacy.

Couples who test out to Competitive/Cooperative would do well to consider whether or not they really want to get married. Or, if they feel they must get married, they should consider just how they are going to meet their mutual need for distance. It is not usual for married couples to maintain separate establishments, but I would not hesitate for a moment to recommend this to a Competitive/Cooperative pair. It could lengthen the effective life and functioning of the relationship.

33

Dominant-Submissive/Cooperative/ Competitive: Turning Molehills into Mountains

This all-embracing interactional pattern, the one that might be expected to be the most rewarding of all, is, somewhat surprisingly, one of the more troubled patterns and one of the most difficult to treat. These nuclear pairs (they represent about 5 percent of the pair population) are usually in a mess. They are mixed up, and the very richness of their interaction seems to add to their problems. They do not know how to make constructive use of the tools at their command. In some ways, they resemble a child who has so many toys that he does not know which one to play with.*

---

*Friendships that fall into this pattern, however, are usually utterly satisfactory and rewarding. The molehill-into-mountain aspect does not seem to enter the picture with friendship pairs. One of the most beautiful games I have observed was played by two high school sen-

The Gilberts were such a couple. Molly and Phil played the Train Game in every possible way, exploring it carefully and logically. There was nothing chaotic about their approach. Molly was a gifted painter; Phil was a C.P.A., very busy and very successful. Molly complained that his work was crushing their life. He spent long hours in his office and brought work home to do nights and weekends. Clients were continually coming to the house to go over their tax problems with him. Molly complained that Phil let his work run him to the point that they had no time together. Her other chief complaint was that she had no time for herself and her painting. She was preparing for an exhibition and it was important to her to have the requisite number of works to display. She was very depressed when they came to see me, because her household duties left her too little time to paint.

Very shortly after they started therapy, Molly was weeping when she came into my office. Phil had just told her in the waiting room that he would not be home for dinner that night. Why was Molly so upset? She said this was the kind of thing that happened over and over again. She could never count on their having an evening together. Phil said that wasn't true. And as evidence, he took out his pocket diary and showed her that he had been home for dinner every night the previous week.

---

iors in front of a group of school psychologists. The girls had been best friends all through school. They sat down, started to play competitively, then gradually moved around to explore every aspect of the game, playing in all three patterns. There was something thrilling about seeing two friends confronted with the game and working through the three major patterns. Their graph was a concrete representation of friendship.

So why *was* Molly so upset? She had complained earlier that she did not have enough time to paint. This would give her time.

Molly suddenly worked up a fury. "I'm stuck with all that goddamned housework," she shouted. "I want Phil to get off my back. I want to paint."

"All right," I said. "You have a deadline for this exhibition. What do you want Phil to do between now and your deadline?"

"I want him to get off my back," she screamed. "I want him to stop draining me emotionally!"

"What does that mean?"

"I don't want to have to make the bed," she said.

There was a silence. All that fury over making a bed? Then Molly laughed. "It sounds ridiculous, doesn't it. But I really don't want to make the bed or cook or clean. I want to be able to concentrate on my painting."

I looked at Phil.

"Okay with me," he said. "I'll eat out. Or I'll bring something home from the delicatessen."

That seemed satisfactory to Molly. They both agreed to work things out this way for the next month until Molly was ready for her big show. But why had she gone into such a tailspin when Phil had said he would not be home for dinner that night? Wasn't that exactly what she wanted—more time to work?

"Yes," she answered confusedly. "But it's always his work. His work is coming between us."

So here was another area that had to be cleared up. It was true that Phil was overloading himself. He agreed that he should cut down and said he would try to arrange things so that he would be around more by the time Molly was ready for her exhibition. In the meantime, they both said they would synchronize their schedules to make as much time for each other as they could. It seemed to work. Molly finished her paintings for the show, and Phil managed to cut down on some of his work. As they did this both were calm and cheerful.

But a few weeks later, it was the same scene all over again. Molly was extremely depressed. Phil was sullen and angry. The problem? The same old thing about time: Phil was working too hard, and Molly didn't have time to spend in her studio. All the new insights they had gained seemed to have flown out the window.

We went over the solutions that had eased their tensions just a few weeks ago. And they agreed that they would try to work out a routine: Molly's needs for close companionship and also for time to paint would be met and Phil's needs to have his wife more nurturing and understanding would also be met.

Again their life seemed to straighten out. But then, the cycle would repeat. The time-and-work problem would erupt again, and they would be back where they had started.

Molly could not free herself from her Dominant-Submissive dependency on Phil long enough to allow the Cooperative interaction to introduce order into their lives. At the same time, she was extremely competitive with her husband. She wanted recognition for her painting, which she equated with the financial rewards Phil got for his work. One reason she worked so hard on her painting, not the chief one of course, was to "show" Phil that she was important in her own right.

And Phil's reactions were almost the mirror image of his wife's. He was competitive with her. He was jealous of the fame she was beginning to earn from her painting.

His way of competing was to take on more and more work and make more and more money—something Molly's paintings would never do. At the same time, he had to dominate. He could not resist criticizing the way the house looked and felt it was her duty to keep the house clean, have good meals for him when he came home, and in general be the model housewife.

When this was spelled out to them over a number of sessions, they professed to understand the dynamics of the situation. It was significant, in view of the chief characteristics of this pattern, that their lives were fairly satisfactory in other areas. They had no sexual problems, except that they could not find enough time for sex. And they liked each other. It was only the problem of divided time that came up over and over again, sent them to the brink of despair, and could not be resolved. Time was truly the only important problem in their lives. It did not seem insurmountable, but they were not able to solve it in two and a half years of therapy.

Another couple who played the same way had the same kind of problem of turning a molehill into an insurmountable mountain. This couple had been married for fifteen years. The husband had had an affair ten years before. It was long over when the wife found out about it, but she could not live with the idea. I was startled when I learned that her husband had been the one to tell her about it.

"Why did you tell your wife about that affair so many years after it was over and done with?" I asked.

"No real reason. I got drunk one night," the husband said. "We had had guests for dinner. I'd had a little too much to drink. After they left, my wife and I were having a nightcap, and my tongue just ran away with me. I didn't want to upset her. I didn't mean to. I honestly don't know why it even came up. But I don't think I'll ever hear the end of it. That was six months ago and it's still stuck in her craw."

He was right. His wife was furious. She couldn't think about anything else. She had blown up this ancient history out of all proportion.

The marriage, which had been relatively happy, was now on the rocks. It was very difficult to help this woman see her husband's old affair in perspective. She kept dwelling on it the way some people can't stop scratching a mosquito bite although they know this can lead to an infection.

The problem in this case was exactly the same as in the case of Molly and Phil—to break up the pattern that was causing the couple such distress. In neither case was there ever a question of terminating the marriage. This never came up. Each couple had come to me for relief from the tension created by one problem that had been allowed to assume disproportionate importance in their lives.

This triple-patterned interaction is the healthiest of all the hybrids, but it is very difficult to treat couples who fall into this category. Incidents that would be disregarded by other pairs, possibly less happy pairs, are turned into tragedies here.

In neither of the cases I have outlined was the stumbling block in the relationship truly insurmountable. Both could have been solved easily and efficiently by most husbands and wives with a reservoir of good will toward each other. But with this group, while there is usually plenty of good will, there is a blindness that keeps them from seeing their problems in true perspective.[26]

If I were counseling an about-to-be-married couple whose Train Game play had graphed out to this particular pattern, I would advise them that they must recognize this tendency to magnify molehills. And if they ever find themselves trapped in such a situation, they must help each other realize that it is a characteristic of their interactive pattern—and nothing to wreck a marriage over. I would advise them to help each other maintain a true perspective when problems seemed to be getting out of hand. Forewarned is forearmed.

34

The Chaotic Eighth

This least-represented of all patterns is not truly a pattern. It is exactly what the name implies—chaos, a lack of order, confusion. There is no pattern.

Some people at first confuse the Dominant-Submissive/Competitive/Cooperative pattern with the Chaotic Eighth. But there is no similarity, because couples in the Chaotic Eighth have no organized approach. The lack of discernible pattern in their play is reconfirmed when one listens to the tape of a nuclear couple who play the Chaotic Eighth: They have no plan; they don't know what they're doing.

This anarchic way of play is extremely rare—only about 1.5 percent of the cases I have seen. Among happily enough married couples it is probably even rarer, or even nonexistent.

It may be that this is a transitory state for some couples. There may be cycles of interaction that move from one of the pure patterns or the hybrids into chaos for certain periods. It will take a long-term study to determine this.

Fortunately, treatment of this group is not at all impossible. Therapy consists of a very strong intervention, of giving the couple a structure within which to interact.

I have gone so far as to make a timetable for some couples:

"At ten in the morning, you will go to the supermarket. At twelve you will prepare lunch. At two you will have a nap. On Saturdays the two of you will go apartment hunting."

I mention apartment hunting because some of these couples seem to have trouble understanding where their home is. One couple I treated who married rather late in life had a very difficult time in coming to terms with the fact that they were sharing a home. The woman moved in with her husband, but he kept running the house as he had when it was a bachelor establishment. She felt like a guest, and she did not dare interfere with his old routine. She became so distressed that she moved back to her old apartment.

At this point her husband became very upset. He could not understand what was going on. They were referred to me by his doctor. When they played the Train Game, they were all over the place. They had no idea of what they were doing.

This was reflected in the way they were living. They had no idea of how husbands and wives set up housekeeping together. I gave them a lecture about each other's rights and responsibilities as if they were teenagers. I spelled out such facts as the wife's right to rearrange the kitchen to suit her convenience, and to redecorate the bedroom; I pointed out that the husband could keep his den exactly as he wanted it.

After a very short time they were living in harmony. Their "graduation" Train Game graph showed a strong Dominant-Submissive pattern with regular Flipflops, and this seemed to suit them very well.

Another couple, a young couple, were living with their

in-laws. Again, it was a question of not knowing where home was. The husband did not feel comfortable with his in-laws. He never felt that he could walk into the kitchen and look through the refrigerator. His wife liked living at home, where her mother did all the work and she had no responsibilities.

Therapy was directed toward helping the wife understand that she should take on responsibility for her own home. This was the couple to whom I gave an apartment-hunting schedule. And this helped. As soon as they got into their own place, everything calmed down. And their final play-through of the game turned out to be Dominant-Submissive/Cooperative with not a trace of the former chaos.

Treatment is not always successful; but for the most part, chaotic couples seem to clutch with great eagerness at any order that is introduced into their lives. Anarchy is simply not a productive life-style.

The Piersons would have been appalled if anyone had called them anarchists. They were registered Republicans—and practicing anarchists. Only one law governed their life together, and that was, "There shall be no law."

Their two daughters were away at college. When Ralph and Veronica consulted me, they said they had been looking forward to this period of their life. They had often talked about the "second honeymoon" that would be even better than their first. No longer inexperienced newlyweds, they had been through a lot together, had raised a family, achieved financial security. Now they were ready to be a little selfish, to spend their time enjoying themselves.

But that was not the way it worked out. Their second

honeymoon was hell. Veronica nagged, Ralph sulked. Every trip they took was cut short because they could not stand each other's unrelieved company. The uninhibited sex life that they had looked forward to now that they had the house to themselves was a disaster, at best, a perfunctory exercise. Veronica was always too tired, too busy, too mad, or too something for sex. And Ralph, after a number of rebuffs, lost his interest—and his erections.

"Some second honeymoon," he complained bitterly. "She won't and I can't." Veronica said, "He's impossible to live with." Ralph said, "I don't know what she wants." Yet, they insisted that they loved each other. Each assured me there was no other man, no other woman.

After the interview, they went to the testing room, where they played the Train Game. The results fed back to me by the computer were astonishing. They had seemed like a moderate, sensible, practical couple, but their private life was chaos. The game showed that they had no mutual plan, did not cooperate, but did not compete either. There was no leader, no follower. Their play was like a series of blind stabbings at this, that, and the other. The Piersons had no idea what their life was about. They played the Train Game one way and another and still another. And not once did they seem to understand what they were trying to do in the game. The result was complete chaos.

When I saw my first Chaotic graph, I thought it might be indicative of mental disturbance or possibly lack of intelligence, but this is not generally the case.[27] The Piersons are as representative of the chaotics as any couple in that tiny splinter group. I considered them to be emotionally stable and of normal, possibly high-normal, intelligence. But when set a task to do together—playing the Train Game for example—they floundered like people who have lost their equilibrium. There was no logic, no pattern, no coherence to their play.

I knew that the Piersons must have had other orderly modes of interaction at their command. Ralph would not have been the successful lawyer he was if he had not been able to think logically, if he had not been able to deal with clients in an understanding manner. Veronica had brought up two children successfully and was involved in community affairs. Their interactions with other people must certainly have fallen into other patterns.

Order had to be imposed before this relationship could go anywhere. In treating Chaotics, one has to step in and supply a focal point for their life. They may change the focal point later, but at the moment they need something to rally around. They cannot keep interacting forever in this absurd helter-skelter manner.

It turned out that all their married life Ralph had been struggling to conform to a set of rules—unwritten rules, unexpressed rules, rules that he learned existed only after he had broken them, that indeed existed only because he had "broken" them. One particularly illuminating example of how this worked was the Piersons' "daffodil argument." It had taken place just a few days before they had made their appointment with me and had been the triggering episode in their decision to seek help.

A shipment of bulbs had arrived from the nursery and had to be dug in for spring flowering. Ralph spent all morning planting them. But when Veronica came back from her shopping and saw where Ralph had put them, she was very upset:

"Why did you plant them there? No one will ever see them. That's a crazy place to put daffodils!" She got increasingly furious as she talked. "You should have put them over there," she stated. "Anyone would see that that's the natural place for daffodils."

So Ralph Pierson, sweating and resentful, dug up all the bulbs, smoothed over the earth and then dug them all in a second time on the opposite side of the lawn.

This was typical of their interaction. It was one big guessing game. Would Ralph do what Veronica wanted? Or would he make another mistake? He always felt that he was on trial, but he didn't know what for. This applied to their lovemaking, their social life, their vacation plans, even to the choice of a restaurant or a film just as much as it did to the decision on where to plant the daffodils.

I pointed out the obvious—obvious, that is, to everyone except the Chaotics: If Veronica had participated and said, "I think the bulbs should go over there on the south side of the house," Ralph would not have had to guess, to plant and replant; there would have been no cause for that particular hassle. I also pointed out that if Ralph had felt strongly that the bulbs belonged just where he had dug them in, he could have said so. His arguments might have convinced her. Her arguments might have convinced him. Or they could have compromised and divided the bulbs between the two areas.

The Piersons looked at me in astonishment. Such a possibility had never occurred to these very intelligent people. The way their life unrolled, the whole episode could have been enacted the following week with nearly identical results. It would have opened differently, because Ralph would have said to himself, "Okay, you got into hot water last week when you planted the bulbs on the north side. This week, plant them on the south side. That's where Veronica wants them." But he would still have been guessing. And probably guessing wrong. Because this week, the rule might be: Daffodils should be planted beside the patio. Ralph would not know what the rule was until he had broken it.

So even with Chaotics, there *is* a structure, a rule, no matter how weirdly scrambled. In the case of the Piersons, the rule they lived by was anarchy. It could be summed up as: "Our rule is that we have no rule."

It did not take the Piersons long to realize that the "no rule" rule had been governing their interaction ever since they were married. Neither Ralph nor Veronica wanted to take the initiative in proposing rules. Veronica (as in the "daffodil argument") formulated rules after the fact, and Ralph spent his time trying to figure out what her decision had been. But they never explored a potential problem beforehand.

After several months of therapy, they played the Train Game again. It was obvious that both had benefited from their recent insights. Ralph started working out a more rewarding way to play. He tried several approaches. In a sense, although Veronica had not asked him to do this, his actions were the result of her command—not an expressed command, rather a nonverbal order. Her message was, "I'm not going to do it. You do it." And Ralph got the message. Ralph's actions were agreeable to Veronica. They both started winning.

This new-found ability to work together encouraged me to think that they might eventually master not just one but two patterns of constructive interaction: Dominant-Submissive and Cooperative, both of them logical and orderly, a far cry from the Chaotic Eighth. But that was still in the future; their graph was now definitely Dominant-Submissive; the parallel lines wavered a bit, but there was no doubt about it. The seeds of this pattern had always been there because of Veronica's unconscious tyranny that had led to the rule, "We have no rules." But now the rule was understood, and Veronica wanted Ralph to work out the solution.

It is tempting to speculate how the Chaotic interaction came into being. How did it happen that Veronica was the one who established the "no rule" rule? Or did she? Was it perhaps Ralph who was so timid or resentful or insecure that he had set up a "vacuum" between them? And since vacuums demand filling, Veronica had stepped in and established the rule of anarchy?

At this point, it is impossible to answer these questions. Yet I am certain that if I had tested the Piersons before or in the early days of their marriage, I would have uncovered the same Chaotic pattern of interaction. I could have shown them exactly what they were doing. Would they have changed? I suspect they would have, because they were so responsive to therapy-induced change. Today, I would not hesitate to step in with any young couple about to be married who exhibited the Chaotic pattern and explain to them the need for establishing some order in their lives. I would not even hesitate to advise them how to establish this order, just as I did with the Piersons. This would save that hypothetical young couple years of grief, for the Chaotic pattern rapidly develops into an enormously distressing way of life.

A couple could accept or reject my advice, but the very fact of accepting or rejecting would entail some joint, coherent action, something that usually has to be imposed upon the Chaotics. Once it is, they tend to accept it.

35

A Matter
of Informed Consent

The Train Game, with its built-in ability to diagnose and classify patterns of human interaction, may be the most efficient tool that exists today for checking the rapid deterioration of marriage and the family. Divorce or separation in more than one marriage out of every three is ample evidence of that deterioration.

In earlier centuries and until recently families were held together by many social, economic, and emotional "glues." Sexual mores were more rigid; divorce was rarely condoned; marriage was an economic and social institution, not a romantic one; and the range of emotional movement available to each member of a nuclear pair was far broader, not only because of available outlets in the extended family, but also because of the more accessible, intimate community contacts that existed less than half a century ago. More people were available to a husband and wife, more people who played a meaningful role in the partners' lives and offered opportunity for significant interaction. These safety valves diffused much of the stress and tension that existed in some nuclear pairs, such as those who fell into the Dominant-Submissive or Cooperative patterns, for instance. Today these "glues" have either disappeared or weakened. Marriage as an institution seems to be falling apart.

I believe marriage must be saved. In a changing world it is still the only institution that offers individuals the necessary emotional security, the love, the appreciation, the easy intimacy, the mutuality that is needed to face an increasingly lonely and impersonal world. It is an emotional fortress. And a good marriage is the warmest, most nourishing, most healthful environment that exists for rearing children.

Marriage not only must be saved but I am convinced it *can* be saved.

Recognizing patterns is the first step in strengthening and improving pair interactions. My hope is that society can use the Train Game to increase our knowledge of human interaction, strengthen good marriages, and, if not prevent, at least alert couples to the risks of destructive ones. I am optimistic enough to believe that few men and women will march blindly into a future that is booby-trapped with emotional time bombs.

If we were to succeed in promoting more marriages with potentially constructive interactions and in preventing some that are potentially destructive, it would have the almost immediate effect of eliminating many of the tensions and stresses that an unhappy union imposes on the members of a family and on society at large, and the divorce rate would undoubtedly be arrested, possibly even take a significant plunge. There would not only be fewer divorces but fewer one-parent families, fewer children in trouble, possibly fewer families on welfare. The emotional climate of the nation could be changed within a generation.

I believe we are today on the verge of a breakthrough

that will make this possibility a reality. With the cooperation of the New York City Marriage License Bureau,
couples applying for marriage licenses in the Borough of
Queens are being invited to play the Train Game and
take part in a longitudinal study that has been set up to
follow a large sample of nuclear pairs for at least a
decade, with good fortune for a full generation. I hope
that similar long-range studies will be instituted in other
sections of the nation in the near future.

Within the span of a generation, our prognosis on the
future of any nuclear pair should be even more detailed,
because we shall by then have more knowledge and more
refined data as a result of the following up of these large
samples (necessarily including well-mated as well as ill-
mated couples) for a meaningful number of years. We
will have learned what circumstances, if any, significantly
alter the patterns of interaction. We will have become
more sophisticated about assessing the quality and
meaningful lifetime of marriages that follow the Divorce
Route. We will have become aware of minor fluctuations
that may exist in interactions that have not appeared in
our observations up to the present. When this series of
longitudinal studies is completed, I would guess that we
would come close to 99 percent reliability in predicting
the futures of tested couples.

I consider this a reasonable estimate because once
people have studied the characteristics of the eight patterns of interaction, many can recognize the more
straightforward ones with a fair degree of accuracy. Patients and former patients routinely tell me that they try
to analyze their important interactive relationships with
a view to improving them. Almost every day I hear some
statement like, "You know, I have a real Dominant-

Submissive relationship with my wife, but with my secretary, it's Cooperative. And with my mother-in-law, it's Competitive."

Recently the *New Yorker* magazine, in a tribute to the late Anna Magnani, the magnificent (and tempestuous) Italian actress, wrote: "She never found any man she wanted who was strong enough to weather the storms she broke daily over his head. . . . From everyone close to her, including friends and relatives as well as lovers, she demanded complete submission, and perhaps for this reason her happiest, longest-lasting domestic relationships were with small animals." When this article appeared, I had several calls from colleagues and patients eager to tell me they had categorized Anna Magnani's relationships as falling into the Dominant-Submissive/Competitive Pattern. I explained to them that this was only one side of the equation, one facet of the interaction; more detailed knowledge of this actress's relationships would be needed to draw detailed conclusions.

Nevertheless, given an ability to identify the less complicated versions of some patterns and given the knowledge that interactions may differ from relationship to relationship, it is sometimes possible for a nonprofessional to perceive some of the pitfalls as well as some of the rewards inherent in a given dyad. If the hazards are predictably stressful, a couple may want to alleviate them with preventive therapy, rather than gamble that they might be able to avoid remedial therapy at some later stage when misery has already set in.

Pairs who suspect that their interaction falls into the Divorce Route variation of the Cooperative pattern or into the Cooperative/Competitive hybrid pattern may want to confirm their suspicions by playing the Train

Game. In such cases, a competent professional may be able to help the nuclear pair to handle the stress constructively, perhaps even to shift the pattern to a more bearable variation.

I must emphasize, however, that nonprofessional "guesses" are just that—guesses. It is extremely easy to be misled about the true nature of an interactive relationship. I have reported in previous chapters how I have often found that my own initial impression turns out to have been quite wrong once I have in my hands the interaction graph printed out by the computer. In the early days, there were times when I suspected that the computer had analyzed its input incorrectly. But this was never the case. In every instance, the true interaction was exactly that portrayed by the graph. The misleading, first impression was false—a kind of red herring that would have distracted me from the truth for months of ordinary therapy without the diagnostic insight offered by the Train Game.

Must a couple take the Train Game test in order to predict the future of their relationship? Yes. At the moment, I know of no other way to secure this information so vitally necessary for stable relationships. And despite the truly astonishing number of correct readings of their interactions that patients are able to make, I must point out that they also jump to an equally astonishing number of erroneous conclusions.

For instance, in the case of the Scrappy Mouse, the husband was convinced that this was a Dominant-Submissive relationship in which he was dominant and his wife submissive. And my first impression corroborated this conviction. The truth was quite different; it was a Competitive relationship, and one in which they were fairly evenly matched, with the wife having a slight edge. I can recite dozens of such cases in which the surface structure was misleading.

The answer then is yes, the Train Game is a necessary diagnostic tool for determining the interactive pattern of a dyad. I hope that the present study at the Marriage License Bureau will lead the way to the realization that every couple contemplating marriage should take this diagnostic test just as they submit to a Wasserman test before being issued a marriage license. Over 80 percent of the couples who have been asked to volunteer have played the Train Game and been eager to participate in later phases of the project.

The fact that it is increasingly easy to get divorced is not a sufficient answer to the problem of marital discord and distress. The problem is that it is too easy for couples to get married in the first place.

If you want to get a license to drive, you must be of a certain age, be able to read and understand various signs and signals, and be able to see adequately. Besides passing tests to show all these capabilities, you have to demonstrate that, even though you're not fully experienced, you can actually drive a car.

Nothing like such a set of requirements exists in order to get married. If you are under legal age, a parent can give permission. Think of it: parental permission wouldn't be enough to enable you to drive or to get you into an X-rated movie—not under any circumstances. But it is enough to get married.

The single most important impact of the Train Game upon marriage is that it has made possible a significant shift of focus. The underlying pattern of interaction between two people embarking on a committed intimate relationship can now be accurately determined. Up to now we have been limited to methods that are directed toward each of the individuals involved but that give little or no information about how these two particular individuals are going to get along *together.*

This shift of focus opens up important possibilities that can profoundly alter the present deteriorating state of marriage and family relationships. It makes it possible for engaged couples to base this most important determination on *informed consent.* This is in striking contrast to the current process, in which the decision to marry is supposed to be based on an ill-defined set of feelings called "love," which human wisdom has long recognized as being, among other things, blind.

In no other aspect of human endeavor is total blindness to what lies ahead regarded as a positive criterion. Men and women generally want to have some foreknowledge, some means of anticipating what lies ahead of them, so as to make whatever preparations may be necessary.

"Look before you leap" is a universally accepted axion, yet when it comes to getting married, the wisdom has been inverted to "leap before you look." No wonder that divorce is skyrocketing, families are breaking up (and down), and that, increasingly, young couples are living together before getting married in order to get some experience about what lies ahead.

While you must have had some driver's education and demonstrate that it has been absorbed, there is no educational procedure for getting married. You not only don't have to prove that you know anything about it, you don't need to know *anything.* The only requirements are that you not have active syphilis and that you can nod your head or give some other sign indicating "I do." (As a matter of fact, if you give no affirmative sign at all, that will be interpreted as acquiescence.)

The driver of an automobile can do harm to himself and others, and it is therefore reasonable that he should have to prove his ability to handle such a vehicle. A couple getting married can do each other, themselves, and their offspring untold harm, yet that is treated as a matter of no concern. And a bad marriage can affect generation after generation. Not only may the original nuclear pair lead what must be considered wasted lives, but the neurotic fallout even on their children's children is incalulable. Just as genetic counseling could have prevented the agonies of hemophilia down the generations of the much intermarried royalties of Europe and Russia, so could interaction counseling prevent much of the emotional distress that besets so many branches of some family trees.

In my view, this is a matter of the utmost concern, not only to the individuals involved, but to society as a whole, and I believe that those individuals know it, even if society doesn't appreciate the fact.

The importance of the Train Game lies in the multidimensional possibilities that it opens up to alter this abysmal situation. The recognition of patterns of interaction that are well established and can be objectively identified by the time a couple becomes engaged gives couples information about themselves that they ought to have. They may choose to ignore the information, but I would expect that most of them would want to have as much of it as possible and to consider its implications. Having done so, some would go into marriage without concerning themselves further; others would want to discuss the implications with trained professional counselors. Such therapy would be preventive, coming at a time when the final commitment has not yet been made, rather than reparative, which is what now happens with one-half of the couples who report that they are unhappily married.

The Train Game could prevent thousands upon thousands of disastrous marriages if engaged couples took this test as a matter of routine and paid serious attention to its findings. I say "could" prevent, because the diagnostic findings of the Train Game should never, absolutely never, be used as anything more than a guide to self-knowledge for an engaged couple. Once they are given the information as to the probable course of their intimate interaction, then it should be left strictly up to each individual pair to decide how to use this insight into the future.

Relationship patterns form early. Their character is easily established and defined by the Train Game. The rules that govern interaction are usually operative at the very beginning of any relationship, since "falling in love" is often a case of meeting an individual who complements one's own rule system. But this is not sufficient in itself to "guarantee" a successful marriage, as we have learned from studying the gross frictions inherent in the Dominant-Submissive pattern. Some rule systems or interactive patterns simply do not hold up in a long-term intimate relationship; other rule systems are so overpowering that they become jails in which a couple is imprisoned, rather than a structure that shelters and nurtures. And then there are those systems that with a minimum amount of change and growth can meet a couple's changing needs over the years satisfactorily enough.

Interaction patterns are not fixed and unchanging. They have their own developmental history. We need to know much more, especially how these evolve as couples move from being a pair to being parents in a group that has three or more members and that then again decreases back to a twosome as children grow up and separate from home to become members of their own nuclear pair.

Am I suggesting that we computerize love? Not at all. That would be an impossible—and useless—task. I am suggesting that we become actively aware of the fact that eight patterns of interaction are possible within nuclear pairs. (A nuclear pair, as I explained in the first chapter, consists of any two people who have an intimate relationship.)

To reiterate, the Big Three "pure" interactions among the eight patterns are:

1. *Dominant-Submissive:* This is the most stressful, but also the strongest of all relationship patterns. Dominant-Submissives rarely divorce. And it is an elemental pattern; there is usually a tinge of the Dominant-Submissive in every relationship.

2. *Cooperative:* This interaction represents society's "deceptive ideal." We tend to romanticize cooperation and consider it a highly civilized form of behavior. But, in fact, this pattern is usually based on fear. The partners are scared of not being loved, of being left alone, so they concentrate on not getting each other upset, on not rocking the boat. They rarely fight, or if they fight they do it ineffectually—because they are so fearful of the consequences. These marriages tend to become rather boring in time, and there is a high percentage of extramarital activity in this pattern. But the partners function effectively and coexist with relatively little friction.

3. *Competitive:* This is the rough-and-tumble relation-

ship, the one with the most excitement. It can be ex-
hausting. The partners often reel with emotional fatigue.
If the competition goes on too long without respite and
is too strong, each will retreat to a kind of enervating
trench warfare. The most successful Competitive pairings are those in which the partners focus their competition outside the nuclear pair. By introducing an element
of cooperation, they can decide to team up against the
outside world. If they succeed in channeling their competition, these relationships can be very rewarding, with
never a dull moment.

The patterns that I have named the Minor Four represent the various combinations possible of the Big Three.
These hybrid patterns are often troubled, but insight
into a couple's interaction can often dissipate the stress
and tension. These patterns are:

4. *Dominant-Submissive/Competitive:* This is a difficult relationship. One factor that causes trouble is that it constantly involves a shift between a complementary relationship (Dominant-Submissive) and a symmetrical one
(Competitive). In one phase the partners are interacting
in a diametrically opposite manner; in the other, they are
duplicating each other's interactions. The shift seems
hard to tolerate. Nuclear pairs in this pattern often manifest the worst traits of both patterns. Shifting from one
mode of interaction to the other, they get no peace. The
one "blessing" is that these pairs, unlike the pure Dominant-Submissives, have some capacity to change when
their lives become intolerable.

5. *Dominant-Submissive/Cooperative:* This is another pattern that involves a constant shifting back and forth between a complementary interaction and a symmetrical
one. But since the Cooperative mode of interaction is

low key and rather conciliatory, this pattern tends to be somewhat less destructive. If the Cooperative reasonableness outweighs the Dominant-Submissive rigidity, all is well with these nuclear pairs.

6. *Competitive/Cooperative:* This doubly symmetrical pattern is a study in contradiction, with a built-in self-destruct mechanism. The pair shifts from cooperating to competing, and back and forth ad infinitum. It's an excellent pattern for friendship, but in a marriage, it's a sign of sure trouble ahead. One odd characteristic of this pattern is that couples who fall into it have space problems—they love each other, but cannot stand very much togetherness. It's the ideal pattern for a traveling salesman and his wife, or an airline stewardess and her husband.

7. *Dominant-Submissive/Cooperative/Competitive:* These couples, like those belonging to the previous category, display a unique characteristic: They tend to get hung up on one problem, usually time-related, and let it ruin their lives. They make mountains out of molehills. If they can be brought to understand that this trait is their Achilles' heel, they can work to add perspective to their relationship.

The eighth pattern is really no pattern at all. I call it the *Chaotic Eighth,* because it is chaos. Complete chaos. And yet, there is one rule that governs it—anarchy, or rather, the rule is "There shall be no rule." This is sometimes a transitory interaction. It is usually easy for these couples to transform this chaos into a more ordered form of interaction if an outsider intervenes forcefully. Fortunately, it represents only 1 percent of pair interactions.

A great deal of resistance exists against analyzing and predicting the interactive structure of a nuclear pair. During the last two centuries, and especially during the last half century, an unrealistic, romantic set of expectations has grown up about the marriage relationship. Marriage has become the key to happiness, the only fulfillment, and the major social obligation. Even today, when marriage is falling into some disrepute even with some professionals, unmarried individuals, whether living singly or in a pair relationship, are still the stepchildren of society—not outcasts, but not quite accepted either.

We have been led to accept a romantic dream, an unrealistic dream, a dream which, if actually true, would be a nightmare, like living as characters in a continuing television commercial. Marriage is an arrangement, the best we have been able to come up with, for providing the security necessary for rearing children, for meeting emotional, physical, sexual, and economic needs. And it can work. But there is no perfect marriage. Today, because of society's fling with romanticism, men and women enter marriage expecting perfection. When they do not find it, they become intolerant, feel cheated, look elsewhere for the perfection they miss. But to create a perfect marriage, one must first create two perfect individuals. This has not yet been achieved.

This romantic expectation is symptomatic of a failure in our educational system. While we require training for professions, we require no preparation at all for the most vitally important profession of all—marriage. When a young person embarks on a career in medicine, for instance, it is with the expectation of engaging in work that will be satisfying, of helping others, of advancing knowledge, of making a good living, but not first and foremost of being "happy." Nor does the lawyer, bookkeeper, painter, journalist expect to be "happy" in his chosen field. Neither should a man or woman expect to find the bluebird of happiness in marriage. Happiness exists, of course it does—and satisfaction, and many rewards. But so do frustrations, irritations, anger, and a host of other unpleasant emotions. This is the human condition.

At its best, marriage offers most partners more fulfillment, satisfaction, and happiness than does an unmarried life, but it demands cooperation, flexibility, good will—all the components of tolerance—and work: exactly the qualities necessary to succeed in any calling. If young people about to enter upon marriage could correct their false expectations, drawn mostly from movies, television, magazines, and other packaged versions of the American dream, they would be less disappointed with the realities of marriage.

When couples who have come to me for marital therapy are ready to leave treatment, I make it clear to them that they must not expect to live happily ever after. The purpose of restructuring a relationship is not to achieve the perfect marriage or total bliss. I explain that I expect them to have arguments, fights, frictions, some psychic estrangement at times, but that I believe they can know how to handle such episodes effectively now, that they will be able to deal with their problems and get on with the business of living instead of playing out their married life with the needle stuck in the same old irritating groove.

My aim as a therapist is not to solve all my patients' problems but to help them learn how to solve their problems themselves. They will always have problems. Life *is* problems. And the very solving of them can bring a couple closer than anything else. I believe that if people were taught how to deal with interactive problems *before* marriage,* they could look forward to a more satisfactory relationship.

The very fact that a Dominant-Submissive couple or a Dominant-Submissive/Competitive couple knew they were taking a certain calculated risk, that they were entering into a potentially abrasive union, would make them more competent in handling marital issues. It would help them reduce the risk factor. They would be able to recognize the stress points in the hidden structure of their marriage and sense when too much pressure was being applied to these points. If such a couple were not able to effectively shift the focus of interaction by themselves, they would understand that this was not the end of the world, that they could seek professional help before the frictions became established as a rule of life. Other couples whose pattern showed that divorce was a probability could ponder whether the relationship would prove rewarding enough for each of them to take the risk.

*I look forward to the time—not too far in the future, I hope— when high school classes in "Family Living" will stop emphasizing sexual compatibility, which is only one facet of the marital relationship, and will instead concentrate on teaching young people about the eight patterns of human interaction, a far better preparation for marriage. In its proper context sex education is worthwhile; taken by itself as a subject, it gives undue emphasis to the purely physical aspect of marriage, ignoring the emotional and many other aspects of the relationship. I also foresee the day when the Train Game will be routinely employed by personnel departments to identify optimally effective staff relationships and to select creative task forces and committees.

It is important to understand that no Train Game prediction is a "sentence" handed down by a computer "judge." People change. As they change, the structure of their relationship may shift. The introduction of a child into a dyad changes the focus of interaction and multiplies the interactive possibilities, just as the departure of a child for college or marriage again shifts the focus and narrows the interactive possibilities.

I would like to ensure that each engaged couple has a chance to understand these matters and to think through the future of their relationship based on the knowledge of their interactive pattern. I would like to have each engaged couple provided with access to unbiased, unemotional advice about their interactive pattern so that they would have an opportunity to think deeply about the realities of their future life as a pair.

The marital relationship is too important as the basic unit of our entire social structure to allow it to go virtually unattended, as has been the custom up to now. Above all, it is a matter of allowing those who are entering into marriage to do so with their informed consent.

The family is not disappearing, nor is marriage going to be displaced by other forms of relationships and living arrangements. Modifications are both possible and necessary, but the family has proved to be the most adaptable and adaptive of all our institutions. It has withstood onslaught after onslaught of every conceivable type throughout the history of mankind. But the probability that it is going to survive does not imply that it should go on staggering blindly into the future.

Properly viewed, the Train Game can provide an opening to vast new changes in the affairs of mankind.

Probably the ideal system, as I envision it at this time, would be to require each couple contemplating marriage to take the Train Game test at least six weeks before a marriage license would be issued. This period would be considered their "psychological engagement," a time during which they would individually and together explore their feelings about the future, about the predicted pattern of their particular relationship, the human atom to be. Such a couple should then be able to give informed consent to their own union after having weighed the pros and cons of their interactive pattern. Society owes them this information. And they owe society their informed judgment.

Scientific Appendix

The following notes, which are keyed to the text for easy reference, are an expansion for professionals and other interested persons of some of the ideas in the book, though they are not essential for an understanding of it.

1. *(Chapter 1, page 5)* The concept of the human atom represented by the nuclear pair gained particular significance while I was studying a fascinating human "trace element"—marriages composed of identical twins married to identical twins. It occurred to me that such quaternary, i.e., four-membered, marriages were structured like the alpha particle of an atomic nucleus. The alpha particle is composed of four nucleons, two electrically charged protons and two uncharged neutrons. The quaternary marriages consisted of two men and two women. Rare as such marriages between two pairs of identical twins may be, I found that Dr. Charlotte C. Taylor, a psychologist, had over a number of years collected information on twenty-five such quaternary marriages, primarily from newspaper and magazine articles. Her findings ap-

peared in *Acta Geneticae Medicae et Gemellologiae,* 20 (1971): 95–113. Nor was Dr. Taylor's list complete. Two characteristics about these groups were particularly illuminating. They tended to live together, either in a single house, a two-family dwelling, or next door to each other. And there were no disjunctive breakdowns among them, that is, in no instance did one couple stay married and the other break up. Either both marriages continued or both were terminated.

The nuclear pair of husband and wife can be viewed as remarkably similar to the nucleus of the atom, which mainly consists of two types of particles, neutrons and protons, collectively spoken of as nucleons.

Within the atomic nucleus, neutrons and protons move about only in *allowed* orbits and obey the Pauli exclusion principle. Actually, the orbits of a paired neutron and proton are slightly different, and these very intimately related orbits can be occupied by only one proton and one neutron. Some protons and some neutrons live alone, are single, having no partner of the other kind.

A very powerful *nuclear* or *meson* force acts between neutron and proton. It is most powerful when they are close together and becomes negligible at greater distances. This little understood yet powerful meson force appears to be analogous to the force acting between the partners within nuclear marital pairs.

Nucleons bump into one another, and these collisions have significant effects upon the structure and the energy of the nucleus. The details of these collisions are complex, but they certainly resemble a dance and can be said to be part of the social life of the nucleon in the nucleus.

For the reader who is interested in a more detailed yet popular description of the nucleus I recommend *The Heart of the Atom: The Structure of the Atomic Nucleus* by Bernard L. Cohen (Garden City: Doubleday, 1967).

2. *(Chapter 1, page 7)* The basic format of the Ravich Interpersonal Game/Test derives from the Acme-Bolt Trucking Game. The former is three-dimensional whereas the latter is two-dimensional.

Figure 1 is the diagram used by Professors Morton Deutsch and Robert M. Krauss and their associates in various conflict and conflict-resolution studies. The important features are the same as those of the Ravich Interpersonal Game/Test.

Two vehicles start at opposite ends of the map. Each has two paths by which to reach its destination. One is a short *Direct Route;* the other is a long, winding *Alternate Route.* Part of each one's Direct Route is a shared *Common Section.* If the vehicles, traveling toward each other in opposite directions, meet at any point along this Common Section, a *collision* occurs. When this happens, both vehicles stop moving. One or the other or both can reverse from a collision, or both can stand still, head-on.

Two barriers are located near either end of the Common Section. Each player controls a *barrier.* The barriers can be closed or opened. If a vehicle is traveling toward its destination on the Direct Route, it cannot pass a barrier that is closed.

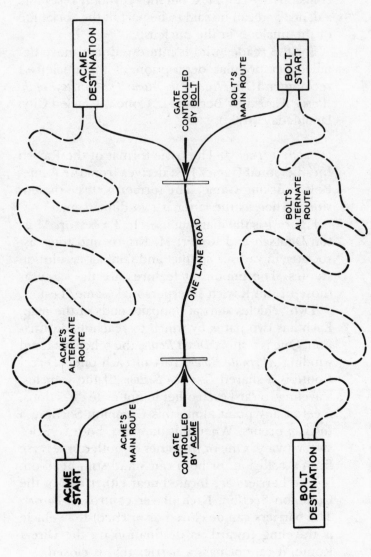

Figure 1. The Acme-Bolt Trucking Game (Deutsch and Krauss).

There are no barriers on the Alternate Route, and no collisions occur if one or both vehicles are on the Alternate Route.

Vehicles can change from one to another route by returning to the starting point.

Figure 2 shows the three-dimensional Ravich Interpersonal Game/Test. The Direct Routes are physically separated but electronically joined. The two sides of the table are divided by a panel. The players can see each other's faces but not the other person's side of the table.

Each player has a control panel (Figure 3). There are two route-selection buttons, one for the Direct and one for the Alternate Route; a switch that moves the train forward, in reverse, or stops it; and two barrier buttons, one that closes and the other that opens the barrier controlled by that person on the other's track.

3. *(Chapter 1, page 7)* For many years, I have been aware that our therapeutic contacts with marital pairs come about usually only when serious discord has developed. Our knowledge of patterns of interaction are largely derived from studying marriages and families under these circumstances. While we find considerable evidence in many couples that the pattern of interaction has been essentially consistent throughout their relationship, we don't have the type of hard evidence that is needed.

It is only by studying the developmental history of the relationship patterns of couples that the fundamental information can be accumulated.

Figure 2. The Ravich Interpersonal Game/ Test (RIG/T3).

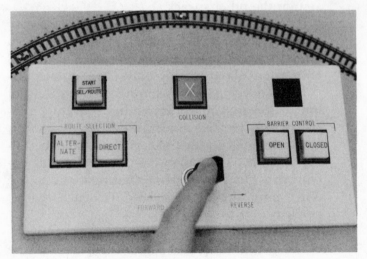

Figure 3. RIG/ T3 control panel.

Several natural points in time suggest themselves. While it would be of interest to have information even earlier, the time when couples apply for a marriage license is the earliest one at which it is feasible to carry out testing on a broad scale.

I attempted to interest the director of the Marriage License Bureau in New York City in this project in 1971. Two years later, with the help of a colleague, Dr. Richard Rabkin, contact was established with Mr. Herman Katz, who is its director, and also the Clerk of the City of New York. After reading the literature, and several meetings, including a visit to New York Hospital, Mr. Katz agreed to an exploratory study, which was inaugurated at the Queens County Marriage License Bureau under the auspices of New York Hospital-Cornell University Medical College. The deputy director in Queens, Mr. Robert Whelan, and his staff have been most cooperative. Here couples applying for a marriage license are asked to volunteer for a long-term research project that will analyze the couple's interaction before marriage and at regular intervals from then on in order to provide a more extensive observation and a further refinement of data on patterns of pair interaction. Many couples have volunteered. Funds are being sought to permit this project to be continued and expanded.

4. *(Chapter 1, page 11)* The use of electric trains as a means of probing such a sensitive and significant subject as marital relationships was, for several years, the basis for ridicule. No better means

seemed to exist, however. My own concern about the matter ended when I learned that one of the most significant series of investigations in nuclear physics was carried out by Henry G. J. Moseley, who also used toy trains to investigate structural characteristics of atomic nuclei. His work provided the basic experimental confirmation of Mendeleev's Periodic Table of the Chemical Elements. It is generally believed that Moseley would have been awarded the Nobel Prize for his work had he not died in action during World War I.

5. (*Chapter 2, page 13*) In order to avoid confusion over terms, it is necessary to draw several distinctions. *Patterns of interaction* refer to the behaviors of two intimately related persons that occur in sequence over a sufficient time span. In the RIG/T situation, the pattern of interaction of a particular dyad is defined by its behavior between the eleventh and the eighteenth trips in the Train Game. There are eight clearly defined categories of patterns of interaction, each having several subcategories. (See note 14 and table on p. 253

An *interaction* is defined as the behavior of a particular dyad during a single trip. Interactions are therefore subunits that are components of patterns of interaction. Each interaction involves the three either-or binary decisions made by each person on a particular trip. These three binary decisions form a unit, the *ternary decision complex.* A ternary decision complex is composed of the three decisions as to whether or not the barrier is closed, which route the person starts his or her train on, and if the train moves only forward or reverses.

For each member of the dyad these three decisions are interrelated, and they are also interconnected with the ternary decision complex of the other person.

There are sixty-four different kinds of interaction possible. While this number derives logically and mathematically from a situation involving two individuals, each of whom has three binary decisions (mathematically represented as 2 to the sixth power, 2^6), it was not arrived at on that basis. Rather, it came about through the sudden realization that the basic structure of an ancient Chinese sacred book, the *I Ching,* or the *Book of Changes,* exactly corresponded to the RIG/T situation, as well as to the basic structure of the modern computer.

The method by which the complex data created by two people taking the RIG/T is transformed into *ternary decision complexes* and into *patterns of interaction* has become inextricably combined with the Train Game. The Ravich Interpersonal Game/Test is the instrument with which interaction is probed, and the derived data is organized and ordered by the *I Ching* transformation method. In the latest stage of the instrument's development the two have been literally electronically fused.

How this came about is an interesting story, one that is central to the theme of this book.

It took almost eighteen months to build eleven models of the RIG/T2, the second manufactured development of the Train Game. These instruments were exact duplicates of each other.

During the time it took to develop RIG/T2, I

began to think about using a computer to process the complex data that was derived from each test procedure. Essentially, we were measuring the length of time and the frequency with which certain events occurred. In order to comprehend this data we were using graphs to show trip-by-trip changes. These graphs were themselves quite complex if all of the desired data was put onto a single sheet, and they became diffused if the different variables were placed on separate graphs. (See Ravich, R. A., "The Use of an Interpersonal Game-Test in conjoint Marital Psychotherapy," *Amer J. Psychotherapy* 23 [1969]: 217.)

I contacted several computer programmers but found them to be of no significant help. Then one day a remarkable advance occurred when I suddenly recognized that the basis of a computer program exactly compatible with the RIG/T2 had been developed more than three thousand years ago and is contained within the ancient Chinese sacred book the *I Ching*.

The *I Ching* had been on my shelf for many years. I had picked it up in a paperback edition because of a general interest in Chinese culture and philosophy but had found it almost incomprehensible. Then one day a patient who was taking a course in Chinese history and culture was telling me about her teacher, who had edited one of the many editions of the book now available. After she left I was scheduled to go to a meeting but I nonetheless felt impelled to look once again at the *I Ching* that had been on my bookshelf for so long.

I recall picking it up and opening to a page near

the middle and then skimming back and forth in the book. Its basic organization was now immediately clear. The central portion of the *I Ching* consists of sixty-four chapters, each headed by a geometrical symbol made up of six lines. There are two types of lines in these so-called *hexagrams,* one type, known as *yang,* being a solid line ————, and the other type, *yin,* being a divided line — —. The sixty-four hexagrams heading the chapters are all the possible permutations and combinations of those two types of lines within a six-line symbol.

Each hexagram is composed of an upper and a lower *trigram.* There are eight permutations and combinations of three *yang* and *yin* lines. The trigrams within a hexagram are viewed as interacting with each other.

The trigrams also have names and stand for a number of things. I was especially struck by the fact that among the various designations given to the trigrams was family membership—father; mother; oldest, middle, and youngest son; oldest, middle, and youngest daughter.

It was immediately apparent to me that the *I Ching* hexagrams and trigrams were a potentially very useful way of organizing the complex data of the RIG/T. Essentially, the solid line and the divided line corresponded to a yes/no, true/false duality, or, in computer language, the binary symbolic numbers 0/1. In the RIG/T, each person had to make the three binary choices. Viewed this way, the time intervals and frequencies that we had been using assumed lesser significance, being behavioral manifestations of the more fundamental decisions taking place within each person and also between them as an interactive decision-making unit.

In the *I Ching* hexagram, the lines are numbered one to six, starting from the lowest line, and are of differential significance, the central line of each trigram being most important. (Initially, I did not take sufficient notice of this particular feature, but I came to realize its importance later on.)

I followed this same procedure, relating each line of each trigram to a specific decision (see page 253).

I immediately applied this new method of organizing the data of the RIG/T to a case that had been both very complex in the graphs I had been using and difficult to understand in therapy. I found that a pattern of remarkable clarity emerged when I did so. It was immediately helpful to the couple.

It is difficult to convey to the reader or even to oneself the excitement of discovering a solution to a complex problem carefully worked out in what may be the oldest book known to man. There may be other ways of solving the problem that confronted me at the time, but I certainly had no idea as to how it might be done, nor did I even know where to look for help or whom to turn to.

Yet here I found on a single page showing all sixty-four hexagrams the basic information that I needed to know. The hexagrams were a visible analogue that could be used to show all of the possible decisions that two people could manifest

Trigram	Subject	Line	Decision	I Ching Symbol	Binary Number	Behavior
Upper	B	6	Direction of motion	*Same as below*		
		5	Route selection			
		4	Barrier use			
Lower	A	3	Direction of motion	– –	0	Forward
				——	1	Forward-reverse-forward
		2	Route selection	– –	0	Alternate
				——	1	Direct
		1	Barrier use	– –	0	Open
				——	1	Closed

in the course of taking the RIG/T on each trip. (See Ravich, R. A., "A System of Notation of Dyadic Interaction," *Family Process* 9 [1970]: 297.)

When one reads the legends bearing on the formulation of the *I Ching* hexagrams and the writings that accompany each hexagram, as well as the commentaries, there is a sense that somehow it evolved out of a game and was then applied in the broadest possible way to all life situations.

In the process of adapting the *I Ching* hexagrams as the basis of an analogue illustrating the decision-making behavior of human dyads, that is, couples, I made a number of modifications, all of which I later realized existed in the *I Ching*.

For example, it became apparent that for each of the three lines of the trigram, one further piece of information was needed beyond that provided by a strict binary system. Instead of depending solely upon ———(1) and — — (0), another symbol (2) was needed. This is provided for in the *I Ching*, which distinguishes between *moving* and *nonmoving* lines. I utilized the symbol (2) in order to characterize specific modifications of (1).

Lines	Meaning of (1)	Meaning of (2)
1 and 4	Barrier closed	Barrier closed second
2 and 5	Starts on Direct Route, finishes first	Starts on Direct Route, finishes second
3 and 6	Forward-reverse-forward	Forward-reverse-changed to other route-forward

By applying this method of ordering the data to a few cases a remarkably clear and comprehensible graph could be made showing exactly how the two individuals had interacted with each other over the series of trips that comprised a test. The previously complex graphs were reduced to two lines that formed geometric patterns that were an analogue to what had taken place in the course of the couple's interactions, and in their joint decision-making processes over time.

It was an extremely tedious task to transform the raw data into the trigrams and then into graphs but I was quite certain that it could be easily done with the aid of a computer.

The next time I met a person familiar with computers and data-processing programs I told him that I thought I had found a basis for writing a program using the scheme of this old Chinese book. Once I explained it by showing him the hexagrams, there was no resistance but rather amazement. For the ancient Chinese had used exactly the same techniques as the designers of the internal processing mechanisms of the modern computer. (A number of writers have become aware of this in recent years. I believe that I may be the first to have consciously used this for scientific purposes. If others have done so, they have not acknowledged the *I Ching* as their model.) The basic symbols are provided by circuits that are either open or closed, and these are arranged in clusters of six circuits. Just as with the *I Ching*, the computer is organized around an 8 x 8 matrix. The *I Ching* symbols ——— and — — much more precisely represent the closed and open electronic circuits than do (1) and (0).

A computerized data-processing program was developed based upon the *I Ching* transformations. It was reasonably satisfactory, but there was some intrinsic error in the formatting of it that showed up in about 10 percent of cases. Together with Dr. Peter Hogan, who has a RIG/T2 in his private office, I tried to find some way to overcome this defect. Our efforts were cumbersome and inelegant.

I finally decided to go back to the *I Ching* and see whether the same problem might have arisen in the course of its development. Sure enough, there was evidence that it had, and the solution to the problem was quite apparent after a short time. By following the solution indicated in the *I Ching,* the deficiency was elegantly eliminated.

Since this successful second utilization of the *I Ching* method proved so precise, I have been convinced that the full importance of the analogue of the hexagrams has still to be appreciated. Although this is a detail that some readers may prefer to skip, I want to explore it briefly.

The problem that we encountered was related to the way in which I had originally ordered the ternary decision complexes. I had arranged them according to the relative degree of aggressiveness and passivity. Since I had considered barrier use as the clearest indicator of aggressive behavior and since the first number in the ternary decision complex indicated barrier use or non-use, the ternary numbers were ordered accordingly.

Errors occurred in the relative position of the lines, especially in situations where an aggressive play by one person was countered by more stubborn yet nonaggressive behavior on the part of the other person.

When I returned to the *I Ching,* my attention was immediately drawn to what are identified as governing lines. The text following each hexagram specifies one or more governing lines, as well as another category called constitutive lines. Clearly these are meant to indicate that these lines have added significance. The governing and constitutive lines are not left to chance, as is the differentiation between moving and nonmoving lines. In most hexagrams the second or the fifth line or both of them are the governing or constitutive lines. The second and fifth lines are the central lines of the two trigrams that form the hexagram.

In my adaptation, the middle numerical symbol of the ternary decision complexes corresponds to the second and fifth lines of the hexagrams and designates route selection. Following this idea through, I rearranged the order of the ternary decision complexes by according the middle number primary importance.

The significance of this rearrangement is that it permits the graph to accurately convey the order of finish, the temporal sequence of who came in ahead and who behind, in almost every instance. The occurrence of errors was reduced from 10 percent to less than 0.5 percent by this change.

This particular discovery has been the most powerful single corroboration within my own experience of the usefulness of the *I Ching* as a basis for expressing interaction. It has helped me to recognize that in a wide range of other fields similar processes of reasoning go on. Whether these derive at times from the *I Ching* or merely display the universality of the internal structure of the *I Ching* and of the human thought processes connected with its symbols is a subject well worth exploring.

The use of the three symbols (0), (1), (2) expanded the number of ternary decision complexes from 8 to 27. Twenty, explained and described on p. 61, are shown on each of the graphs that illustrate the text. The full number of possible dyadic interactions on a single trip is 315 rather than 64; however, it is still the 64 hexagrams that are the basis of understanding the structure of interactional behavior by means of the RIG/T.

6. *(Chapter 5, page 31)* In the almost thirty years that have passed since I began to work in cancer research there has been a great deal of ethical and legal debate as to the patient's right of *informed consent.* The American Hospital Association has recently published a "Patient's Bill of Rights," which has been adopted as policy by many hospitals. It includes the following:

    "The patient has the right to receive from his physician information necessary to give informed consent prior to the start of any operation, procedure, and/or treatment. Except in emergencies, such information for informed consent should include but not necessarily be limited to the specific procedure and/or treatment, the medically significant risks involved, and the probable duration of incapacitation. When medically significant alternatives for care or treatment exist and the patient requests information concerning the alternatives, the patient has the right to such information."

No such policy had evolved during the time that I was engaged in cancer research. I myself had strong feelings about the subject then, as now. I believed that individuals had the right to knowledge about what was going on in their own bodies so that they could make appropriate plans.

I learned to "play the game" in those years, but I have since learned a great deal about the subject of game playing, rules of the game, and the structure of relationships. It seems to me that the same issue of informed consent is involved in the process of marriage and that this goes far beyond the ceremonial "I do" uttered by bride and groom.

7. *(Chapter 5, page 37)* It has occurred to me that there is some profound analogy between the carefully orchestrated avoidance pattern of the "Divorce Route" and the game between the living and the dying that I observed between cancer patients and their families. If living is one route and dying another, and the outcome secretly or openly agreed to is separation or divorce through death, then as long as either the living or the dying, or both, avoid the subject, it can never be discussed. Some pairs structure the situation differently, the task being viewed as getting onto the same route. In some instances this means open discussion of the impending loss and separation. These pairs will get as much out of the time they have together as

possible. In a few cases, living together will be rejected, and instead, dying more or less together is the agreed-upon resolution. And then there are those who seek to bridge the separation through séances and other parapsychological means.

8. *(Chapter 6, page 43)* The encouragement that a person receives in the earliest phase and at critical junctures often has a significant influence on the future development of new ideas and methods. I am deeply indebted to two psychiatrists who encouraged me in the course of supervising my treatment of a number of cases—Dr. Philip Polatin and Dr. Joseph Lubart, while I was a resident at New York State Psychiatric Institute and a trainee at the Columbia Psychoanalytic Clinic.

9. *(Chapter 7, page 48)* I have sometimes had the thought that, without knowing it, I have been consistently guided by the late John von Neumann. He was the theoretical mathematician who, together with Oskar Morgenstern, developed game theory. When my interest turned to atomic theory, I found that much of the fundamental mathematical logic of the Copenhagen school of theoretical physics led by Niels Bohr and Werner Heisenberg was the work of von Neumann. And then when I related the *I Ching* hexagrams to the Train Game interaction patterns and found that the modern computer was based upon the same essential matrix, I learned that von Neumann was responsible for much of the logic of today's computer.

10. *(Chapter 7, page 49)* The Amalfi Drive story may or may not be apocryphal. It was told to me by Dr. Krauss, who was working toward his doctorate under Professor Deutsch at the time when the Acme-Bolt Trucking game was conceived. When *Life* magazine published an early article about the RIG/T, they included the story. Deutsch's reaction was one of amusement. He remembered observing the incident, but not that it had any connection with the origins of the instrument he and Krauss designed.

Another source of the Deutsch-Krauss design in my opinion can be traced to several of the experiments carried out by Kurt Lewin as part of his studies in *field theory*. Deutsch had studied under Lewin in his graduate-student days and, like many other social psychologists, was influenced by his ideas and is a disciple of his. On one occasion I pointed out to Deutsch an article of Lewin's in which a diagram of an experiment exactly resembles one-half of the two-person game. He said that he had been unaware of any such relationship.

The role of Lewin in the development of the Train Game is of considerable conceptual importance because of the connections between theoretical nuclear physics and what I refer to as the human atom. Lewin was part of the German Gestaltist school, of which Köhler, Koffka, and Wertheimer were the best-known proponents. Albert Einstein and Wertheimer were good friends. Not surprisingly, Einstein frequently utilized the model of two trains traveling in opposite directions toward each other as a means of explaining the special theory of relativity.

The great Swiss child psychologist Jean Piaget had many discussions with Einstein about the nature of thought and the concept of space-time. There are clearly links between some of Piaget's experimental procedures and the Train Game.

11. (*Chapter 7, page 49*) Bert Brown, who was a graduate student in Morton Deutsch's department, was present when we met. He offered to test the couples and worked closely with me for several years before he moved to Ithaca, New York, where he has taught in the Cornell School of Industrial Relations. His contributions to the development of the first Train Game are important, and some of his ideas are incorporated in the technique used in administering the test.

12. (*Chapter 7, page 50*) "Why trains?" is a question often asked. There are several answers, all contributory in different ways, practical, symbolical, and psychological.

The first electrical engineer assigned to work with me by Scientific Prototype Company was Michaelangelo Rossetta. Mike had much in him of the sculptor and the poet that his name conjures up, and I have always considered that it was my very good fortune to have had his imaginative approach available at the beginning.

Mike and I met at Polk's, on lower Fifth Avenue in New York City, which is probably the largest store in the world catering to the various hobbies.

Having in mind the Deutsch game, which involved imaginary trucks, we went to the "slot-car" section, which occupied an entire floor. As soon as we began to play with the equipment, we realized that these models were incapable of backing up, which was a required function.

We then went to the floor below, which was entirely devoted to model-train equipment. There was no doubt that this field of engineering incorporated the degree of sophistication required. The reasons are clear: model railroading has always kept up with actual railroad developments, largely because the sale of real railroad equipment demanded models. When American railroad engineers originally went to Russia to sell the Czar the idea of building a railroad, they took a working model with them, and the Czar became a model-railroad buff then and there, long before the real railroad was constructed.

The fascination of model trains for adults as well as for children, for women as well as for men, is constantly evident in the total absorption that the Train Game elicits within the first few minutes for every dyad. For several technical reasons there would be advantages to using moving lights instead of actual model trains, but everyone who has worked with the Train Game has reached the same conclusion, that the trains lend a special quality and dimension that should be retained.

The symbolism of the train and tracks appears to be extremely powerful and remains unchanged even today, when trucks and airplanes have taken over much of the function of the Iron Horse. The fantasies that people attach to the trains are amazingly rich and varied, and their impact is often evident in dreams and associations after couples have played the Train Game.

There is also an element of my own personal psychological past involved, as I realized after a conversation with Dr. Murray Bowen, one of the pioneer greats of family therapy. Many people have said that I must have built the Train Game because I was frustrated as a child by not having trains to play with. I must have shrugged that off a thousand times with the response that I did have trains. Bowen, who is a master of the paradoxical approach, put the question quite differently. He said, "I'll bet a lot of people say that you were frustrated as a child by not having trains, and that's why you invented the Train Game. But of course that's not true, is it?" With that he turned away, leaving me for the first time with the question "What is true?" Then I recalled that whenever, as a boy, I set up my trains on the floor of my bedroom in our apartment, my mother would make me take them apart and put them away before I went to sleep. I would sometimes think about making a permanent setup on a board that I could raise to the ceiling at night so that my mother would stop being concerned about my tripping over the tracks in the dark. In addition, a cousin of mine who lived in a big house that I often visited had an elaborate and permanent tabletop setup of model trains in an attic room, and I did envy that constant availability.

13. *(Chapter 7, page 51)* The RIG/T3 is an extraordinarily complex instrument. The technical problems involved in the various phases of its development have been solved by a combination of fortunate occurrences. Extremely rapid advances in the field of electronics made it possible to introduce features that were in my mind from the outset, but were beyond the state of the art of electronic engineering. Within a period of five or six years, technological progress made the impossible possible.

At each stage I have depended upon professional engineers and computer experts and have been very fortunate in the excellence of those who have worked with me. I have already referred to Mike Rossetta, who designed and built the first RIG/T. By early 1969 a U.S. patent had been issued, and the RIG/T2 had been built. More advanced electronics made it an efficient instrument that collected much more data. Richard Doherty, also of Scientific Prototype, was the engineer who built the RIG/T2, and he has continued to be actively involved in subsequent developments.

Eleven RIG/T2 instruments were constructed. Each has had its own fascinating history. One was stolen from the Gouverneur Clinic and still remains unaccounted for.

The latest version, RIG/T3, is the handwork of a brilliant electronics engineer, Curt Stahl, who brought to bear the experience gained in creating the most complex types of electronically controlled military and space equipment. In the process of designing the technical means for altering the parameters of the Train Game, Curt created an electronic analogue of the *I Ching* transformations without knowing that this was the method that I myself had evolved for organizing the data. This provided a fundamental validation of the structure of the instrument and of the method.

The computer programming has been done from the beginning by Howard Radin. When we first began to work together, Howard was still a graduate student at Massachusetts Institute of Technology. The data-processing programs he has developed have been of vital importance to the progress of my work. Integrating the hardware of the RIG/T3 and the software programs in order to make the Train Game and the computer fully interactive is a task of staggering complexity.

Unquestionably one of the most important figures in the development of the Train Game in its present form is Al Merritt of the Service Bureau Company. Ever since I had the idea of processing the data by means of a central computer, Al Merritt has given freely of his guidance and excellent judgment. He brought Howard Radin and Curt Stahl to me, and the entire system would have been quite different—or perhaps would never have existed at all—had he not been so generous in his help and familiar with the problems that confronted me.

14.   (*Chapter 8, page 53*)The English language as well as all the languages of Western civilization are peculiarly lacking in words that accurately and correctly convey interaction. This may be an important se-

mantic reflection of our neglect of the nuclear dyad as an interacting entity having its own characteristics. Ours has been essentially an individual-oriented society.

In order to communicate the subject matter of this book, it has been necessary to use familiar words even though they are inadequate and misleading. I would much prefer to do away with the words used to describe the patterns and use symbols instead. In this respect, I share the feelings of many composers who resist the programmatic names and associations applied by others, or sometimes themselves, to music that they would prefer to be experienced unhampered by the constraints of written and spoken language.

My own preference is to conceptualize three major patterns, identified as D (dominant-submissive), E (equalizing, cooperative, alternating), and F (fighting, competitive). All three ways of interacting are potentially present within each dyad, and thus I always use the three letters together. A pattern of interaction that is manifested is indicated by the capitalized letters, while nonmanifested ways are represented by small letters.

A group of 140 consecutively tested intimate dyads, mostly married couples seen in my private office practice, has been classified according to the pattern of interaction shown during the resolution phase of the RIG/T. The cases came from a middle- to upper-class urban and suburban population. Presenting complaints covered the wide range of difficulties likely to be seen by anyone specializing in the field of marital therapy.

As can be seen in the table below, of the three primary patterns, *Def* is the most frequently encountered in this series of 140 cases, 37 dyads showing this pattern. *dEf* is next, with 28 dyads showing this pattern. *deF* is the least often encountered of the primary patterns, 20 dyads showing this primary pattern of interaction.

A total of 85 dyads (60 percent) showed one of the three primary patterns. Another 53 dyads (38 percent) showed one of the four possible mixed patterns, and 39 of these were in the two categories *DeF* (22 dyads) and *DEf* (17 dyads).

There are four categories of mixed patterns. Three of these categories (*DeF, DEf, dEF*) are composed of two of the three primary patterns. The fourth contains elements of all three of the primary patterns (*DEF*).

Only two dyads in this series showed a pattern of interaction that did not permit them to be readily placed in any other category. These were designated as *def*.

Studies using the RIG/T carried out by others on marital dyads that are "happy enough" indicate that the distribution among the categories is just about the same.

The table below shows the number (out of 140 cases) and percent of dyads that fall into each of the eight designated groups.

Pattern of Interaction	Number of Cases	Percent of Cases
Def	37	26
dEf	28	20
deF	20	14

Patterns of Interaction	Number of Cases	Percent of cases
DeF	22	16
DEf	17	12
dEF	7	5
DEF	7	5
def	2	1.5

15. *(Chapter 9, page 67)* Children may have enormous difficulty in leaving families in which a Dominant-Submissive pattern prevails. It is a powerful magnet, and at least one child is held firmly within the field. Some children in their late adolescence and early twenties will go to great lengths and travel vast distances in their efforts to get away, but they are drawn back into that field. I recall one college junior who had gone to India to study. He was the younger of two brothers. In his absence his parents began very seriously to contemplate divorce. He "went crazy" in the main square of a small Indian city, was picked up by the Indian police, handed over to the American consul, and flown back home, where he was immediately hospitalized. Concern about his behavior had always been the parental pair's major topic of discussion. The customary situation was reestablished by his dramatic return.

It is impossible to explain in this case how the effects of the interaction field can extend over such distances. Everyone insisted that there had been no communication, verbal or written, that could have indicated to the young man in India that he had to come home. Nor was he conscious that anything that he was doing there was going to lead him back home. Quite the contrary, he thought that he was learning a totally new life-style that would get him away once and for all.

16. *(Chapter 9, page 69)* One of the "rewards" of marriage is that it provides an arrangement between two people that enables almost anything that goes wrong to be blamed on the other, who is always conveniently at hand. The wish to absolve oneself of responsibility is quite universal. The Dominant-Submissive pattern of interaction is particularly prone to this.

17. *(Chapter 11, page 84)* It is difficult to be certain whether Glenna was totally unaware. The collision light goes on and off quite rapidly, but the speed with which light travels through space to the retina and the signal is transmitted by the optic nerve to the brain is many times faster. So it is also possible that Glenna actually knew but was not aware that she knew, because she either could not or would not process information that came more rapidly than she was willing to acknowledge it. Other people with the same interaction see the light go on and off, but ignore it—or deny that it has significance.

18. *(Chapter 19, page 135)* The appropriate time for couples to be tested is when they become engaged. At present the time interval between applying for a marriage license and getting married is related to legal measures rooted in concern over venereal disease, specifically syphilis, and its congenital manifestations in offspring. It seems unreasonable

to me that this should be the state's sole concern regarding couples who have decided to marry. A broader perspective would lead to a significant number of changes in how individuals are educated for the vital tasks of marriage, parenting, and family life. Change in the time interval between the decision to marry and marriage itself would be indicated.

19. *(Chapter 20, page 139)* The tester's role is especially emphasized by the distortions of this type of couple. It is, however, a crucial aspect of the RIG/T. Testers have to be specially trained, and many people cannot perform the task. Difficulties arise for the tester, not so much in learning the technical details, but in staying out of the field of interaction, and not being overly affected by what goes on between couples.

Inexperienced testers often find themselves drawn into some kind of interaction with the couples. But for experienced testers there is also an emotional response, more with some couples than others, and not specifically related to the verbal exchanges nor to the duration of the test. After some tests, the tester appears to have something akin to the "bends" experienced by those who work underwater at too great pressure levels for long periods.

The effects are not necessarily negative. Sometimes the experience from the tester's point of view is actually exhilarating. This may not be experienced too often when couples take the test because of marital distress. But if the RIG/T were

to be administered as a routine premarital procedure, more such uplifting experiences would be
reported by testers and might contribute significantly to our knowledge of favorable marital characteristics.

Someday, I am certain, there will be a means of
measuring objectively the psychic force that exists
between people. Until then, the subjective re-
sponses of well-trained testers are of considerable
value.

I am deeply indebted to those who have under-
taken the tester's role and stuck with it. Bert
Brown was the first of these. Joann Clements Slatt
has helped me in so very many ways and has been
the first "professional" in the quantity and quality
of her experience and knowledge. She has passed
her knowledge on to others who have applied it in
the various centers where the RIG/T has been
used.

Those who adapt to the tester's role find it fascinating and rewarding. This has been the experience of those testers who have worked with and
helped me so much: Kathleen Westin and Marge
Rhoades, as well as Gretchen Howerton in Newport News, Virginia, and William Horst in Omaha,
Nebraska.

20.   *(Chapter 21, page 146)* Marital and family therapists
       often have difficulty in communicating with one
       another about their clinical experiences. In part
       this is due to the fact that the therapist who has
       treated a couple or family has to report his own
       observations to others, who are thus getting their
       information as he provides it to them.

For those therapists who use the RIG/T as a guide, the situation is quite different. They can look at the computerized graphs and tables and thus have a shared starting point. I am particularly grateful to a small group of therapists who over a number of years have shared their experiences with me, thereby expanding my own knowledge.

Dr. Edwin Church, in New York, Dr. James Howerton, in Newport News, Virginia, and Dr. Merle Sjogren, in Omaha, Nebraska, are psychiatrists who have had considerable experience with the RIG/T. Michael Rothenberg, a psychologist, was my associate for several years, and the work that he did toward his doctoral thesis was an important contribution to the knowledge of the differential effects of stress upon couples in therapy and "happy-enough" couples.

Joseph Dorflinger, M.S.W., and Wayne Twombley, both social workers in the mental health field in Bristol, Connecticut, have applied the RIG/T in new and exciting areas of training and research, including studies on juvenile delinquency and child abuse.

Earl Rhoades, a minister, has worked with Dorflinger and myself. He has developed a profound understanding of the RIG/T and the data that it yields, as well as a special competence in the technique of the postgame interview.

I have identified the backgrounds of these colleagues to emphasize that the RIG/T, even in its earliest stages, is not confined to or identified with a particular specialty, training, or experience. Actually, it appears to have a particular appeal to therapists and researchers who are especially attuned to patterns of interaction between people, rather than to intrapsychic mechanisms. I believe that this "tuning in" on different channels is very important. The sphere of "between" is a channel that requires specialized aids. Gestalt theorists long ago pointed out that "grounds" are much more difficult to perceive than "figures."

21. *(Chapter 22, page 151)* The subject of testing co-therapy teams is one of considerable interest to professionals. This has only recently begun. Others have been interested in testing patient-therapist pairs and therapists-in-training and their supervisors.

A wide range of potential applications in the business, industrial, and labor-management-relations areas is beginning to be explored collaboratively by me and Roy Walters, a leading industrial consultant.

22. *(Chapter 29, page 190)* Because of the Dominant-Submissives' resistance to change, as well as their resistance to seeking therapy, the percentages of couples in the two complementary/symmetrical patterns who seek marital therapy may be somewhat higher than the percentages of these couples in the population at large. They may actually represent as much as 35 percent of the population. (See footnote, page 69.) The percentage of pure Cooperative and Competitive couples seeking therapy appears to be just about the same as the percentage in the population at large. It is impossible to know the true percentages without a study

of unselected cases. Neither the study based upon couples who responded to a newspaper article seeking volunteer couples who were happily married (carried out in Chicago by Dr. Bernard Liebowitz and his associates under a grant from the Mental Health Department of the State of Illinois) nor the study at the Marriage License Bureau that is based upon volunteers about to marry can provide an adequate basis. The reason is that couples who don't volunteer cannot be assumed to have the same distribution. We know this is so, and indications are that it is primarily because a significant percent of Dominant-Submissive couples will not volunteer, or will withdraw from any study because it will be perceived as threatening to the relationship. Paradoxically, it is the very group that feels most threatened by intervention that is most resistant to any change.

23. *(Chapter 30, page 192)* A number of studies suggest that this difference between the Dominant-Submissive/Competititve and the pure Dominant-Submissive groups may be of considerable significance. In two series of couples in which the alcoholism of one member was so serious as to require hospitalization, all of the couples showed these two patterns of interaction. These studies were carried out at the National Institute on Alcohol Abuse and Alcoholism by Drs. Peter Steinglass and Steve Wolin, and at Silver Hill Sanatarium in New Canaan, Connecticut, by Dr. John Tamarin and Earl Rhoades.

It is my impression that the prognosis for improvement or cure is very different for individuals according to which pattern of interaction exists in their most intimate relationship. Treatment of alcoholism is often discouraging, but this may be partly due to the fact that differences between these two groups have not been previously recognizable.

An analogy may help in understanding the significance of this. Penicillin is a wonder drug because it cures a very high percentage of certain specific types of pneumonia. If these specific types could not be discriminated from among all cases of pneumonia, penicillin would not be regarded as a wonder drug, because it has no effect whatever on many types of pneumonia.

Another small but significant series of observations has come out of the work of Dennis Moore, a graduate student at Wright State University in Dayton, Ohio, who studied families with a mentally retarded child. For reasons that at this point are obscure, almost all of the parental pairs showed a Dominant-Submissive/Competitive pattern of interaction. Moreover, in these families there was not the slightest trace of cooperative interaction.

It is not possible at this early stage to know what this finding means. It is quite unexpected, since mental retardation has not been considered to be related to family interaction. Perhaps the observed behavior is a response to the presence in the family of a mentally retarded child. At present it seems wise to keep in mind the possibility that at least some cases of mental retardation may be re-sponses to the child's environment. Some recent reports have appeared of isolated cases of young people who for years had been institutionalized because of mental retardation and who were found not to be retarded at all.

For thousands of years, there have been reports of children who were raised by wolves. The twins Romulus and Remus, who according to legend founded the city of Rome, were said to have been nurtured by a wolf. But most reports represent such children as being essentially mentally retarded when they return to human society. Why should this be so? Does this merely reflect the lack of human speech, or is this possibly attributable to the pattern of interaction in a lupine family?

24. *(Chapter 31, page 203)* More than in any of the other categories of interaction patterns, this one appears to be a failure of fusion of two separate rule systems, one brought into the relationship by the woman, the other by the man. Instead of the couple developing its own rule system, each partner adheres to the one that is known from childhood, and neither is able or willing to give it up. Thus there is an unresolved, continuing struggle between the two rule systems, and, in a cyclic manner, one is in the ascendence and then the other. Warfare that is characteristically open, with emotional and physical abuse in many couples of the Dominant-Submissive/Competitive type, is expressed in embittered silences that can last for days, weeks, months, or even years.

25.   *(Chapter 32, page 208)* It seems to me that the under-representation of this type of pairing has far-reaching social significance. In many ways our entire social system is founded upon a positive evaluation of cooperation and competitiveness. The capitalistic system is supposed to encourage competition, and monopolistic domination of a particular aspect of the economy is strongly resisted. On the other hand, cooperativeness and fairness are highly valued.

The pairing of cooperation and competition within families would seem to be particularly favorable and favored, yet just the opposite is the situation, indicated by the very low representation of this type of interaction.

There is evidence that couples with this pattern have greater difficulty in getting married. This is suggested by the finding that they have a premarital relationship time span that is more than twice as long on the average than any other group. It may be that couples with this pattern are over-represented among very early divorces and separations. If studies now going on support this speculation, it would suggest that a combination of factors, including the pattern of interaction, economics, and space are involved. Couples with the Cooperative/Competitive pattern of interaction may require more living space than newly married couples can afford, or are supposed to require.

Many people are concerned about animal species that are threatened with extinction and campaign vigorously for their preservation; couples who have a Cooperative/Competitive pattern of interaction seem to me to be similarly threatened with extinction. Yet they are a very necessary group in our society as it is constituted. We might all benefit from a change that somewhat limits Dominant-Submissive relationships and increases Cooperative/Competitives. In terms of spatial requirements, these may represent opposite poles. Dominant-Submissives may need and use somewhat less than an average amount of space, while Cooperative/Competitives must have more than an average share.

26. *(Chapter 33, page 215)* The core of the difficulties that these couples encounter may be related to time rather than space. Many couples have time and timing difficulties in many or all aspects of their lives, sexual relations often being the most distressing one. Partly these difficulties stem from a rather universal misconception regarding time. Each of us has an internal clock, and we assume that everyone else is operating in accordance with that clock or one that is exactly synchronous with it. But time intervals actually are experienced very differently, so that the expected synchronicity is too often lacking.

Couples who interact in the most consistent ways are probably less affected by this than those who are most inconsistent. Swift shifts from one to another and to a third pattern of interaction can all too easily get "out of synch."

There is clear evidence of this in both of the couples described. The Gilberts' problems were related to time difficulties in the present. The sec-

ond couple's trouble was related to confusion between the relatively distant past and the present.

27. (*Chapter 34, page 219*) This is not the case because
two truly mentally retarded people are unlikely to
marry.

When mentally retarded children played the
RIG/T with their parents or with siblings, 10 percent of the patterns were in this chaotic category.
This recent finding, taken together with others,
gives added importance to the question of the connections between the structures within the human
atom, the structures within the human mind, and
structures in general. Are there common structural
features everywhere—in the environment, within
intimate relationships, and within the individual
mind—which enable us to understand and learn
what is going on? And does mental retardation
signify absence or insufficiency of such structures
in human minds?

In bringing the structure of relations into the
foreground, the Train Game not only clarifies a
great deal—it also raises new and intriguing problems, as well as putting old ones into different
frames of reference.

Index

Index